All the Letters I Should Have Sent

Rania Naim

Art direction and design by KJ Parish. Title illustrations by GloriAnne Rose Dairo. Cover photography by God & Man. Published by Thought Catalog Books, a publishing house owned by The Thought & Expression Company. It was printed in the United States and published in an edition of 1,000 copies.

ISBN 978-1-945796-62-3

…the people we loved
and the people who couldn't love us.

…the ones who broke our hearts
and the ones that got away.

…the ones who loved us
and the ones who healed us.

…the ones who made us ask important questions
and the ones who gave us the answers.

…all the people who once came into our lives
and left an impact, left a mark or left a scar.

This book is for you.

To the
People
we Loved
and the
people
who
Couldn't
Love Us

DEAR EX-BOYFRIENDS

Thank you for loving me.

And thank you for leaving me.

Thank you for giving me a taste of everything delicious and a taste of everything sour.

Thank you for introducing me to euphoria and introducing me to pain.

Thank you for being there to hold my hand and thank you for letting me go.

Thank you for being everything and then nothing.

Because of you, I learned to believe in love. I learned that some parts of me are worth loving. I learned that I have qualities that others can appreciate and admire.

Because of you, I learned how to love, how to give and how to compromise. I learned how to make someone a priority, how to share the best and worst parts of myself with someone else and how to be a better person so I can be a better partner. I also learned how to love myself, how to stop myself from crying because of you and how to live without you.

You softened my heart but you hardened my core.

It's like you were all an extension of each other. You didn't fall when I fell. You stayed on the shore while I swam deeper into the ocean.

You all loved me at one point but not enough to stay. Not enough for forever. You all left and came back but you never changed, you were never genuinely sorry. And then it hit me.

I wasn't meant to be with any of you. All you had was potential. All I had was false hope.

You were examples of what to avoid.

You were examples of everything I should stay away from.

Thank you for showing me what I truly deserve.

Thank you for the memories and thank you for the lessons.

You prepared me well for heartbreaks. You taught me how to move on when people leave.

I OFTEN WONDER WHAT WOULD'VE HAPPENED HAD WE STAYED FRIENDS

I have a habit of saying too much, only to regret it later.

I have a habit of being all in or all out.

I don't know how to stay friends with someone I have feelings for. Someone I wanted more from.

But with you, I often wonder if staying your friend would have been better for us. I often wonder if our story would have been different if we removed the weight of feelings, labels and commitment.

Would you have fallen in love with me eventually? Or would I have stayed just a friend?

Because as a friend, I'm less emotional and more logical, so maybe I wouldn't have been so jealous when I saw you with her.

As a friend, I'm brave. I'll text first, double text, call whenever I feel like it and make plans with you.

As a friend, I'm calmer, I'm wiser, I don't care about being the one who cares more or the one who's doing more.

As a friend, I have fewer expectations. I don't get attached too easily.

As a friend, I don't jump in with both feet. I'm more guarded. I take my time and I take things slow.

And maybe this is everything you needed, maybe this is all you were looking for but I acted too fast and pushed you away.

I often regret not being your friend first.

But I also know that when someone likes you, they won't tolerate being your friend, they won't give you a chance to date other people. They'll always show you how much they care about and they won't be afraid.

And that's when I realized that maybe you're afraid and I'm more daring.

I'm a little bit more fearless when it comes to love. A little bit more fearless when it comes to you.

And that explains why you choose friendship and I choose love.

That explains why you prefer distance and I prefer intimacy.

That explains why you keep me at arm's length and I prefer holding your hand.

That explains why I don't want to be your friend and why you don't want to be my lover.

TO MY FAVORITE 'ALMOST'

They think you're mine and I'm yours.

They think there's a love story going on behind closed doors.

They think it's only a matter of time before someone tells them the truth they've been waiting to hear.

We roll our eyes when they joke about us being an item; we laugh at how ridiculous they're being. But deep inside, I'm crying. I'm crying because what you're taking as a joke is what I wish could be real.

We look at them like they're a bunch of fools but maybe I'm the real fool. A fool for you.

And in that moment, I realized that you'll always be an 'almost.' You'll always be something in between. You'll always be somewhere in the middle. You'll always be someone I can touch but can't hold. You'll always be so close yet so far.

So I laugh with you at their jokes and pretend like it doesn't bother me but what I'm really laughing at is myself, because I'm the joke. I'm the one who thinks an *almost* can turn into *forever*. I'm the one who believes that eventually people get tired of almosts and they look for something more definite. But I know better. I know that some people stay an almost forever. I know that almost is another word for *nothing*.

But out of all my almosts, you're the one who meant the most. You're the one who almost made me believe in almosts. You're the one who almost broke my heart.

WHAT IF WE WEREN'T SUPPOSED TO LET EACH OTHER GO?

What if this was a mistake?

What if this wasn't supposed to end?

What if it was just a bump in the road, not a car crash?

What if it was just a phase and we confused it with forever?

Maybe this is why we can't find anyone else. Maybe this is why we can't make it work with anyone else. Maybe this is why we keep running into each other so randomly. Maybe this is why we still can't forget each other.

What if we took the easy way out? What if we should have tried harder?

Because letting go shouldn't feel like a burden, it shouldn't be something you regret, it shouldn't be something that holds you back.

Letting go shouldn't feel so wrong.

Letting go shouldn't be an act against your instincts and it shouldn't be an act against your heart.

It shouldn't be an act at all.

What if we got used to bad acting but that's not the role

we were assigned to play?

What if we were supposed to learn how to love each other instead of leaving each other?

What if we were supposed to learn how to be patient instead of quitting?

What if we were supposed to grow old together instead of growing apart?

What if you were supposed to be the one and I turned you into the one that got away?

Tell me, do you ask yourself the same questions, too?

Tell me, do you sometimes feel like all we needed was a little wind but we turned it into a hurricane instead?

WHY LOVING YOU WAS DIFFERENT FROM LOVING ANYONE ELSE

I'll always love you more than anyone else because you taught me what love is.

Loving you wasn't just a few dates and sweet messages. Loving you was understanding what it's like to live with another human being. It was knowing which side of the bed you like to sleep on. It was learning how you like your eggs every morning. It was learning if you prefer tea or coffee. It was listening to your childhood stories and looking through your old family albums and knowing what it's like to be woven into someone's life.

Loving you was learning how to be kind, how to be soft, how to be thoughtful and how to be understanding. Loving you was letting go of my selfishness, letting go of my mood swings, my pride and my fears.

Loving you was learning how to respect our differences, how to find beauty in your imperfections, how to still be there for you and be your strength even when my world is falling apart.

Loving you was discovering what love does to a woman. Love fuels her sensuality and makes her burst with passion, affection, softness, tenderness, kindness and an infinite ability to give and keep on giving.

Loving you was learning that I could be loved too, with my flaws and imperfections, with my insecurities and my baggage. Loving you was learning how to unload this baggage so I could be light again. Loving you was learning which parts of me I need to work on and which parts of me should stay the same. It was recognizing that love makes me invincible. It makes me a poet. It makes me a force to be reckoned with.

Loving you was learning how to believe in love. It was learning how to trust again. It was learning that love doesn't always hurt. It doesn't always walk away. It doesn't always destroy us.

Loving you was learning that love is a personal choice and I'll always choose love. And if I had to do it all over, I would still choose you.

TO THE ONE WHO LEFT TOO SOON

Do you regret it?

Does it hurt when you see my pictures?

Does it hurt when you read my words?

Do you wonder if my poems are about you?

Do you sometimes write a long message to apologize, then delete it?

Was it me? Was it you? Was it timing?

Was I too hard to love? Were you too scared of loving again?

It's hard for me to believe that you're a bad person because you were so kind to me. It's hard for me to believe that it was all fake because it felt genuine. It's hard for me to believe that you had that connection with everyone because I didn't feel like you were pretending. I didn't feel like you were acting.

Was it so hard to ask me on a few more dates? Was it so hard to ask me a few more personal questions? Was it so hard to text me back to keep the conversation going? Was it so hard to *like* me?

Why am I always the one who's ready? The one who's

willing to stay, the one who's willing to try against all odds and the only one who's willing to fight?

Why am I always the one dreaming and you're the one waking me up?

Why does it begin with smiles and end with tears? Why does it always have to be you against me? Why can't it be *us* against the world?

I hope one day you tell me why you left too soon. I hope one day you tell me the real reason. I hope one day you tell me the truth.

Sometimes I wonder about you. What you're doing, who you're with, why you picked her and if you ever think about me.

Sometimes I wonder if you will ever reach out, just to say you miss me, say sorry or just to hear my voice.

And sometimes I wish you had stayed.

I hope you learn how to stay. I hope you stop leaving.

I hope you learn that staying is the only way to open your heart and stop running. I hope you learn that some people—like me—would've done anything for you to stay.

I hope you learn that there's so much more value in staying than leaving.

I hope you learn that staying doesn't always hurt.

TO THE ONE I CAN'T STOP MISSING

I miss you.

Sometimes I feel like these three words are enough. They sum up the past five years of my life. They sum up my story with you, but if you're looking for more details, then let me tell you exactly when I miss you.

I miss you when I'm alone. I miss your warmth that melted the ice inside my heart. I miss your vibrant energy that could fill even my darkest nights with color. I miss your aura and how it used to fill my lonely nights with life. I miss how I stopped being afraid of the dark when you were beside me.

I miss you when I'm with people. When I look at them and remember you. When I talk to them and hear your voice. When I make them smile and suddenly picture you.

I just miss you.

Missing you has become my habit. My routine. *Because missing you is better than forgetting you.*

Missing you is what reminds me that I can still feel—that I can still love.

And if you think my silence means that I forgot about

you, you're wrong. My silence means I miss you but there's nothing I can do about it. I can't change your mind.

My silence means I still want you but I need to know that you want me, too.

My silence is really a tapestry of all my thoughts, the unspoken words and the repressed feelings that are all ready to reveal themselves the moment you say something.

So talk to me because I have so much to tell you but for now, *I miss you is enough.*

TO THE ONE WHO TAUGHT ME HOW TO FORGIVE

I was furious. I was hurt. I was broken.

I wanted to hurt you the way you hurt me. You brought out my vindictive side and all I wanted was revenge.

I started planning and scheming. I used all my tactics to get even with you. I started thinking about the day I see you drowning in tears and regret. I couldn't wait for the moment I can look at you and say, 'I win.' I wanted to win. I didn't want to be a loser. I didn't want to lose to you.

Then my mom got sick and I had to drop all my schemes and stay by her side. Being at the hospital every day reminded me that life is so fleeting, it can end in a second, *we* can end in a second, *we're all too fragile to be acting like we're better or bigger than others. This life is so transient and it's exhausting to try to win everything.*

I don't want to win every argument. I don't want to break the person who broke me. I don't want to keep seeking revenge so I can satiate my ego. I don't want to lose myself just so I could look like a winner. I don't want my pride to dictate my life.

I'd rather lose. I'd rather let go. I'd rather forgive. I'd rather set myself free.

Because being a 'winner' won't really matter in a moment of weakness, a moment of illness or a moment of defeat when all you need is someone by your side, when you need every prayer you can get, when all you need is love.

I don't want to be alone in a hospital bed. I don't want to be remembered as a vindictive winner or a vengeful loser.

I want to be remembered as a kind soul, a bountiful heart, a delightful spirit. I want to be remembered as the one who loved life too much to hold grudges or spent her best days trying to get even with people.

I want to be remembered as the girl who forgave people and the girl people always forgave.

Because maybe the whole point of anger is to teach us how to be even more compassionate and more tolerant.

Maybe the whole point of life is to teach us that winning or losing won't really matter when it's our time to go; what will really make the difference is how much you loved and how much people loved you and how they'll remember you.

And I want to be remembered as the girl who loved too much, even the ones who didn't deserve it. I want to be remembered as the girl who cared more, even about the ones who never gave a damn, the girl who was generous with her heart, even to those who were stingy with theirs.

So I forgave you. As for the pieces of my heart that you have, you can keep them. I don't want them back.

I still have a lot more pieces to give. I still have a lot more love to spread.

SOMETIMES I WONDER IF MAYBE I
HADN'T DONE ENOUGH TO KEEP YOU

Sometimes I wonder if maybe I didn't say all the words I should have said. The ones that would have explained to you how I truly felt, how much I needed you and what you really meant to me. Sometimes I wonder if I should have filled my moments of silence with more candid and softer words.

Sometimes I wonder if things got harder because I didn't make them any easier. I was scared of getting hurt so I played it safe. I feared opening up and telling you everything so I held back. I was afraid if you knew my weaknesses and insecurities, you'd hold them against me so I pretended to be someone I'm not to impress you.

Sometimes I wonder if I spent the whole time trying to make you trust me that I forgot to trust you back. Sometimes I wonder if I was asking for what I couldn't provide.

Maybe I really didn't do my part as much as I thought I did. Maybe I didn't give my all, maybe I preach about loving too hard but when it came to loving you, I fell short. I backed off. I was afraid of how hard the fall may be. I was afraid I wouldn't be able to get up.

Sometimes I wonder if I'm not as fearless as I claim to be because nothing terrifies me more than heartbreak, nothing scares me more than someone loving me one day and deciding they don't want me the next. Nothing terrifies me more than being so close to someone and then watching them become a stranger again.

Sometimes I wonder if I believe in love as much as I say I do or am I secretly a skeptic. Sometimes I think love is waiting for me to wholeheartedly believe in it before it finds me.

Sometimes I wonder if I wasted all my love on you and if it was ever enough.

IT HURTS WHEN PEOPLE TELL ME IT'S A BLESSING THAT YOU'RE NOT THE ONE

It hurts.

To know that the one my heart chose is the one I needed to stay away from.

It hurts when people tell me that I'm better off without you or I dodged a bullet or someone out there is much better for me.

It hurts that God sent you as a lesson; it hurts that you were just a test. It hurts that you're not the final answer.

Sometimes I wonder how I confused you for a blessing if you were a curse.

Sometimes I wonder how a curse can be so pretty, so enigmatic and so angelic.

How did I see you as an angel if you're the Devil?

It hurts when people tell me I deserve better and when they call you a mistake.

It hurts that you were not meant for me and it hurts that we're not meant to be.

I wish there was a way to turn around our fate.

I wish there was a way to make you a blessing that stays, to make you a solution instead of a problem.

I wish God never picked you as an example of who I should avoid. I wish he picked someone else.

I wish I still had a chance with you.

I wish I didn't know any better.

It sucks that when I count my blessings, I can't count you.

It sucks that when I talk about love, I can't mention you.

IF ONLY YOU COULD LOVE ME THE WAY I AM

If only you could love me with my messy mind and my shambolic thoughts.

If only you could love me with my restless heart and my somber words.

If only you could love me with my brutal honesty and my twisted lies.

If only you could love me with my contradictions. The way I love and hate myself simultaneously. The way I get closer but push you away at the same time. The way I can be so weak yet so strong. The way I fall in love with you while I try to guard my heart.

If only you could love me with my baggage, the bruises from my past, the many lives I've lived before you, the little child within me that doesn't want to grow up and the confused little girl that's still looking for answers.

If only you could love me the way I am without making me feel like a burden or a heavy weight or a liability.

If only you could love me the way I love you.

I STILL THINK ABOUT US
GETTING BACK TOGETHER

I've been secretly thinking about you. I've been secretly waiting for you. I've been secretly hoping that one day I'll open the door and you'll be waiting for me outside because you want me again. I've been secretly wishing for the day I get your call and we can talk for hours about everything that happened so we can start over.

I've been desperately waiting for us to start over.

I always believed in comebacks. I always believed in second chances. I always believed in a universe fighting for two people to end up together. Fighting for two people to grow apart so they can realize how badly they need each other.

I always believed in me and you.

But sometimes years pass by and you never show up. I switch phones and I still don't hear from you. I move across the country and I never find you.

Sometimes I wonder what's harder: you not coming back or me waiting for something that will never happen.

Sometimes I wonder what's taking you so long and why you're still not here.

And sometimes I just give up. I try to embrace someone new and think of new beginnings. I try to let you go and focus on someone else but it never works. It never feels right.

And up till now, nothing feels as right as you coming back to me.

Up till now, I can't really love anyone else when part of me is still waiting for you.

Up till now, I'm holding on because I can't figure out how to let go.

IN CASE I NEVER SEE YOU AGAIN

I know we didn't say goodbye but I know this is the end.

I've seen this movie before. I know when it's time to roll the credits.

I know it all too well.

So, in case you never come back, I want to you know that I truly cared.

I want you to know that the first time I met you, I didn't want to leave; I wanted to talk to you all night.

I want you to know that I liked your smile, I liked your eyes, I liked your depth and all I wanted was to hear your story. I wanted to know your *soul*.

I want you to know that the second time I met you, I knew I wanted to see you again, I wanted to be around you more, I wanted to hold your hand.

I felt safe with you.

You made me happy.

You took me out of my darkness.

I saw someone special. I saw someone delicate.

I thought we made sense. I didn't anticipate any plot twists.

But that was my movie and I wanted a happy ending.

But I guess your movie wins, your ending is climactic, your ending is more realistic.

And that's the thing about movies; *they don't always end up the way you want them to.*

And that's the thing about endings; they can sometimes be sad.

They sometimes end in tears.

They end and they don't always have a sequel.

A LETTER TO THE ONES I HAD TO LET GO

Let me tell you how I did it. Let me tell you how I got your ghosts out of my system.

I stopped thinking about you late at night when I was alone wishing you were there so I could talk to you. I started talking to my best friends. I started reading. I started writing. Because I realized they've all been there for me in all the ways you weren't and they're still here with me but you're gone.

I stopped staring at my phone when something good happens hoping you would say something and I stopped staring at it when something bad happens tempted to call you and tell you about it because you never wanted to celebrate with me and you never wanted to give me a shoulder to cry on when my tears wouldn't stop falling.

I remembered that I couldn't count on you to make me smile when you're the ones who made me cry.

I stopped comparing anyone I met to you. I stopped believing in the same spark that burned me—the flames that turned to ashes.

I'm done living in this illusion I've created with you and I'm ready to face my new reality without you.

And finally, I stopped thinking that you'll come back one day. I stopped wanting you to fight for me because the truth is, I don't want a fight—love shouldn't be about fighting and it shouldn't be a war. It shouldn't be a battle of who cares more and who's going to fall harder. It shouldn't be about winning and losing.

And if it is, then I don't want it. Maybe I'm just a dreamer but I believe that love should be easy, it should be simple and clear. It shouldn't be all questions and games and it shouldn't leave you wondering or waiting.

And maybe I'm just a dreamer but I believe that love should be magic and it should leave you in awe.

TO LOVE,

I still don't know your address. I still don't know where your home is. I still don't know which country you reside in but I know you're near. I know you're close. I know you still have a place for me.

I know eventually, I'll belong to you. I know we are meant for each other but until then please take it easy on my heart. Don't break my heart anymore, don't lead me to the hearts of all the wrong people or the hearts that don't beat for me.

Just be soft, be gentle and be honest.

Don't lie to me anymore, don't leave me alone, don't lead me on, don't be a replica of the real deal. Don't get me excited about everything that's not you. Don't let me see you as a dream when you're a nightmare.

Don't run way when I search for you.

I'm tired of walking behind you; I want to walk beside you. I'm tired of sleeping alone; I want to sleep knowing you'll be there in the morning.

Please don't leave me in the dark anymore, please don't take the light away.

We both know that I've been looking for you all my life

and we both know that the day I'll find you, I'll cherish you forever.

So find me—find me, for you have a home in me. The home that you've been looking for, the home that can raise you right and nurture you and the home that will make you forget about all the homes that kicked you out. All the homes that didn't want you.

I'm the home that will not make you question what the hell is wrong with love or the world—I'm your shelter from the rain.

You and I are meant to be.

You and I will heal each other because if I'm the remedy then you're the *cure*.

To The
Ones Who
Broke
Our Hearts
and The
Ones Who
Got Away

TO THE ONE WHO MADE ME HOPE FOR MORE

I remember how it all started. Late-night calls and fancy dinners. Long conversations under the stars, baring our souls to one another like we were one with the universe. It all felt so heavenly. So euphoric.

It felt like a dream. And maybe it was because shortly after, you woke up. You woke up and you stopped being there. Your texts got shorter and your calls were dry. I could feel your distance, I could feel my heart breaking every time I heard your voice and it wasn't the same. You're not the same. *We* are not the same.

I knew it was the beginning of the end but I was trying so hard to change that ending. I was trying so hard to make it a happy one.

But you like sad endings and sad movies. You like tears and goodbyes. You like things that you can control, things that you can replace and darling, I wasn't one of them.

I was forever in your world of temporaries. I was a priority in your world of options and you just didn't know what to do.

You made me hope for so much more. You made me see a future with you. You made see stars in the middle of the dark, but eventually you dimmed the light you brought into my life.

I just want to let you know that even though you made me hope for so much more, you also made me settle for so much less. Even though you said you loved me, I realized that you don't know what love is.

Because love doesn't know how to give in doses, love gives unconditionally. Love doesn't take things back, love gives freely. Love doesn't just make people hope for more, love gives them what they're hoping for and more.

In learning to love you, I learned more about what love is and what love is not.

And in making me hope for more, you made me hope for much more than what you were willing to give me.

You made me hope for much more than you.

I WANTED IT TO BE ME

I wanted to be the one you're holding in front of everyone.

I wanted to be the one you're kissing when your friends are around.

I wanted to be the one you look for in a crowded room.

I wanted to be the girl who walks with a smile on her face because her man is in love with her.

Instead, I was the girl who had to see it all backfire, the girl who had to watch you choose someone else.

I was the girl who had to leave wondering why she's never the one.

I was the girl who went home and covered her sheets in tears.

I was the girl who fell for someone who didn't catch her.

It kills me. When I remember how quickly you forgot me.

It kills me. When I remember how you said you weren't ready for me but you made yourself ready for her.

I wanted it to be me. The girl who made you ready. The girl you couldn't afford to lose.

TO THE ONE WHO TAUGHT ME THAT SUMMER SKIES CAN TURN CLOUDY

It was a beautiful summer.

You, me and the ocean.

Kissing. Storytelling by the beach. Dancing under the moonlight.

It was a bright summer.

Full of laughter. Full of sunny promises and happy songs. It was a dream.

You and I were wild. We weren't that young but we sure acted like it.

We didn't see anyone else. We didn't even meet anyone else. It was just us. It was paradise.

But summer ended quickly.

When things stopped being easy and started getting real.

When I looked at you and you saw that I was falling in love.

When I stopped swimming and started drowning.

When the waves were too high and I couldn't surf anymore.

Suddenly, the skies turned gray, the sunlight went away and the weather got colder.

Suddenly, it felt like winter.

Then you left.

And ever since then, I can't enjoy summer anymore.

Because it always reminds me of you. It reminds me that just because it's sunny doesn't mean it won't rain.

Just because it's summer doesn't mean you shouldn't prepare yourself for an unexpected storm.

You taught me how to always be prepared for storms. You made me expect rain during sunny days.

You taught me that summer can be heaven but it can also turn into hell if the heat is too much.

And it can burn you.

ALL I WANTED TO DO WAS LOVE YOU
BUT I PUSHED YOU AWAY INSTEAD

I'm sorry I responded to all your texts on time. I answered all your calls and I said yes to all your dates.

I'm sorry I opened up to you, I let myself be vulnerable, I trusted you even though I didn't know you well enough but I was comforted by your presence and the compassion in your eyes.

I'm sorry I wasn't guarded with you like I am with everyone else. I'm sorry that there was something about you that made me want to forget about everything that happened in the past and all the men who broke my heart and to instead focus on you.

I'm sorry I lived in the moment a little too much—it's like I had a feeling it might not last.

I'm sorry I wanted you to have no doubts about how I feel or question my intentions for you. I'm sorry I thought you were tired of women breaking your heart and playing you. I'm sorry I wanted to reassure you that I'm not like them and you don't have to question anything with me. I'm sorry I wanted to make you feel like you're the only one.

I'm sorry I *chose* you. I'm sorry I didn't keep exploring my options or playing games with you. I'm sorry I didn't play hard to get or act like I'm not interested. I'm sorry I decided to lead with my heart and be honest and genuine with you. I'm sorry I wanted to love you like you've never been loved.

But I'm also sorry that you wanted to stay on the shore and you couldn't swim any deeper. I'm sorry you wanted a storm when I wanted a lighthouse. I'm sorry you wanted to stay broken and I wanted to heal.

I know I keep saying sorry for things I shouldn't be apologizing for, for feelings that were real, for the way I loved you but I am not sorry because I was wrong; I'm sorry because I was so right and you couldn't see it.

I feel sorry for you because you gave up forever for something temporary.

TO THE ONE WHO WASN'T READY

Did you know that I wasn't either?

Because I was a mess and you had your life together.

You had a great job and I was still figuring out what I wanted to do with my life.

You had a stable income and I was barely making ends meet.

You had a loving family and I came from a broken home.

Your life seemed to flow perfectly leaving no room for you to question yourself whereas my life kept falling apart leaving me to question everything I've ever known.

It didn't make sense to me that you weren't ready. I should be the one all over the place. I should be the one scared of ruining whatever we had.

But I wasn't. I wasn't sure of anything else, but I was sure about you.

At a time when all my decisions were wrong, I felt that you were right.

And even though you said you weren't ready, I knew you were.

Because we're always ready for the right ones. We make ourselves ready when we can't stop ourselves from falling.

And that's when you taught me that it's not about being ready, it's about giving someone a chance.

It's not about commitment issues, it's about appreciating the person enough that you don't want to lose them.

It's not about timing, it's about how much time you really want to spend with that person.

It's not about logistics, it's about emotions.

It's about your heart and who it moves for.

And maybe I didn't move yours the way you moved mine. But don't tell me you weren't ready; just tell me I wasn't the one.

Because now I know that I'll never be ready but I'll always jump in with both feet when someone moves my heart.

I'll always find more reasons to stay and fewer excuses to walk away.

Because walking away is easy but trying is brave.

It's brave to say you're ready even when you're not.

TO THE ONE WHO WANTS TO
KEEP ME AS A 'MAYBE'

We've been through it all.

We've been through the confusing phase, the are we, or aren't we? The texting games, the playing hard to get, the meaningless things we did to make each other jealous until we both caved in. Until we both confessed, until one night, *we said it all.*

You said it's been me all along and I said it's always been you.

You said you loved me and I said I loved you, too.

Then you had to leave and I had to let you go, not knowing if you'll ever come back, not knowing if I'll ever love anyone the way I loved you and not knowing if there is anything worse than this feeling, the feeling that everything you ever wanted is no longer yours. The death you experience when you're alive.

The heart that no longer feels anything at all because it wasted everything on you.

But you came back, because something like this doesn't just end, it lives on, it comes back, it's what fairy tales are made of, it's what we secretly live and hope for and it's what we dream about.

Until it was time to let you go again. This time it didn't hurt as much or maybe I just got used to that kind of pain. *The pain of loving someone who will never be mine, the pain of giving someone a chance knowing that they will blow every chance I'll ever give them.*

But I decided that if you want my door to always be open for you then I'll have the key. You'll only come in if I decide to let you back in; you can't show up uninvited anymore, you can't just open my door again without my permission. It's not your call anymore.

But if you decide to come back in, promise that you'll never leave. Promise that this is the last time you'll use distance or time or work as an excuse. Promise that you're ready to do this and do it forever.

Because there can't be any more 'maybes' between us; we've wasted them all.

Because this time, my heart is tired and it just needs to rest.

This time, if you're not all in then you're all out.

This time, it's all or nothing.

This time it must be definite because I can't handle another *'maybe.'*

THE LETTER I WANTED TO SEND YOU
AFTER I SAW YOU WITH HER

I saw her and I finally understood why it never worked out between us.

She's the type of girl who manipulates everyone around her to get them to like her. She's the type of girl who puts on a show people want to watch. She's the type of girl who says all the right things and asks all the right questions so she can make everyone feel that she truly understands them. That she feels their pain.

She's the type of girl who gets what she wants only because she is pretending to be someone else, someone she knows you'll like and respect, someone she knows you'll want to be with but what's going to happen when she takes that mask off?

Will you still be enjoying her show? Her entertainment? Her exceptional acting skills? Or will you long for someone who is real? Someone who makes it easier for you to know what they're thinking, someone who makes it easier for you to trust them and someone who makes it easier for you to differentiate between reality and fiction.

I guess you didn't like my honesty and you wanted to live a lie.

You still want to be challenged even if it means getting

hurt, you still want to wow everyone you know by who you're dating even if you don't get to wow yourself. You still want to be the fixer for someone who is going to break you and you still want the ones who will never truly love you the way you want to be loved.

Seeing her made me realize that I didn't even know you because if this is who you fell in love with, then there was no way you'd fall in love with me.

I guess I blame myself for thinking that people always want what resembles them, someone as kind as they are and someone as loving as they are, but I also realized that some people want exactly what they're not. They want someone who will make them doubt themselves or change who they are and some people only want people who will make their lives harder because they're *addicted* to the pain.

All it took was seeing her to understand why you never fell for me.

All it took was seeing her to wholeheartedly believe that I'm not the girl for you and you're not the guy for me.

I NEVER KNOW WHAT TO SAY WHEN PEOPLE ASK ME ABOUT YOU

I never know if I should call you a stranger. But how could you be a stranger when I know too much about you? How could you be a stranger when I told you my deepest fears and feelings? How could you be a stranger when I still see you and recognize every little thing about you? I still remember all the details. All the memories.

I never know if I should call you a friend. Because we're not really friends. We don't call each other and chat about our lives, we don't talk to each other about who we're dating, we don't meet up for coffee and talk about work and life. We don't talk at all. We just act cordial when we see each other but we don't know anything about each other and maybe we don't want to know because knowing too much could potentially hurt us. I can never call you a friend because to me, you were much more than that.

I never know if I should call you an ex. Because technically we were never in a relationship, at least one that people knew about, we don't have a lot of pictures together, we didn't have romantic getaways or confess our love to each other, but we had something real. We had something that could have been love but it didn't go very far. We stopped. *We paused.* We took ten steps back. And even though you weren't an ex, heartbreak songs still remind me of you.

Even though you weren't an ex, I still miss you from time to time.

I never know if I should you call an almost. Because that's what you were, an almost lover. We almost made it but then I refer to *almost* as something of the past, something that is no longer in my life, something to forget because it didn't mean anything to me. *But you weren't an almost to me, you meant something. I was sure about you.* You weren't someone I wanted to forget and you weren't someone I wanted to let go.

So when people ask me about you, I never know what to say. I don't know how to describe you or describe *us*. I don't always find the right words to tell them how I truly feel. So I just say that we don't really talk anymore and I'm over it but the truth is it all still haunts me, it all still hurts and I still remember it like it was yesterday.

Time hasn't changed a thing.

TO THE ONE WHO DIDN'T WANT TO DATE ME BECAUSE HE DIDN'T WANT ME TO WRITE ABOUT HIM

I wish you had the courage to forget what I do for a living and focus on who I am. I wish you had spent your time getting to know me instead of wondering what parts of our conversation will make it into my next book.

You were trying so hard to avoid being another story and here you are ending up in one of my books, but instead of writing a beautiful story, I'm writing a sad one.

I'm writing a story about fear and how it stops us from taking a chance on something that could have been astounding.

I'm writing a story about the mind and how it tricks us into believing that sometimes the world revolves around us.

I'm writing a story about the irony of life, how you said you admired people with passion and purpose yet you refused to be with someone who *embodied* all of that.

I'm writing a story about the ego and how it gives us a false sense of importance, a false sense of pride that could prevent us from taking a phenomenal leap of faith.

I'm writing a story about a man who was attracted to a woman and her story but decided he didn't want to be in it.

I know I told you I wouldn't write about you. I know I told you I write about those who break my heart or those I'm madly in love with.

But I'm writing about you just because you didn't want me to write about you.

To serve as a reminder that what you resist persists, that once you touch a writer's heart, you'll always be there and they'll always find a place for you in their story.

But instead of having the leading role, you settled for just a random character in my story, an extra, a cameo.

Instead of being a whole chapter, you settled for a page.

And that's the saddest part of our story; I was interviewing you for a role you were so unqualified for.

TO THE ONE WHO BROKE MY HEART
BEFORE ANY BOY EVER DID

To the one who yelled at me for being a foolish kid instead of hugging me and teaching me how to get things right.

To the one who would always tell me to shut up because he thought my opinions were dumb.

To the one who thought he was always right and blamed me for anything that went wrong.

To the one who only loved me when I was quiet and hated me when I was loud.

To the one who didn't know how to keep a home warm and safe. To the one who made home a place to fear, a place to avoid and a place to run away from.

To the one who turned my childish dreams into nightmares.

To the one who failed to be an inspiration, a role model or a pillar.

To the one who made me pack my bags and leave. To the one who abandoned me and left me alone with his ghost and his voice in my head.

You're the reason I push men away. You're the reason I fear love. You're the reason I always ask for more because you gave me nothing. You're the reason I can't trust a man. You're the reason I don't know what a home is.

You're the reason I keep messing up because you never guided me. You're the reason I know pain so well.

Because of you, I don't know what love is. Because of you, I pick the ones who leave. Because of you, I pick the ones who bring out the worst in me.

But that's over now. Now I figured out how to get rid of you.

Because of you, I found a way to bring out the best in myself. I turned you into art. I told the world about you.

You went from being my best-kept secret to something I need to throw away, something I need to get out of my system, something I need to get off my chest—like poison, I needed to detox myself from you. Like a burden, I needed to drop you so I could remember how to walk steadily again.

The world knows you're my poison. The world knows you made me sick.

But the world healed me.

And now I'm happy and you're alone.

You're the sad story, not me.

You can't hurt me now.

The world will save me.

IT'S GETTING HARDER TO FORGIVE YOU

It's getting harder to forgive you every night I come home alone and you're not there.

It's getting harder to forgive you when I need you but I can't call you.

It's getting harder to forgive you every time I feel scared because you were supposed to be protecting me.

It's getting harder to forgive you when I can feel your absence in my life. When I see your ghost everywhere I go.

It's getting harder to forgive you when your memories still haunt me.

It's getting harder to forgive you every time I realize that I shouldn't have to live without you but I do.

It's getting harder to forgive you when you're always the reason behind my tears.

I keep saying it's going to get easier but it doesn't. I keep saying it's not that hard but it is.

I keep saying I don't miss you but I do.

But every time I hope for something more from you and I don't get anything, *I miss you a little less.*

Every time I say that this time you will finally stay, you end up leaving again.

And it's getting harder to keep up with you. To wait for you. To defend you. To believe in you. To believe in us.

It's getting harder to love you again.

It's getting harder to forgive you but it's getting easier to *forget* you.

I'M DELETING YOUR NUMBER
EVEN THOUGH I DON'T WANT TO

I'm deleting your number because I don't want to be tempted to text you whenever I see anything that reminds me of you because everything reminds me of you.

I'm deleting your number because I have to stop myself from scrolling down trying to get to your name and staring at it hoping that by some cosmic spell, you'd finally call me.

I'm deleting your number because I don't want you to be the first person I think of calling when something bad happens. I don't want to keep remembering that I never feared anything because I knew you would help me get through it.

I'm deleting your number because I don't want to call you when I miss your voice. I don't want to have any access to you.

I'm deleting your number because I need to give someone else a chance. I'm tired of shutting people out. I'm tired of comparing everyone to you.

I'm deleting your number because I'm done torturing myself over losing you. I'm done with your maybes. I'm done with your uncertainty. I'm done with your games.

I'm deleting your number because I'm looking for love and that's something you're still confused about.

I'm deleting your number because you couldn't make me the only girl.

I'm deleting your number because it's time to delete you from my life.

MAYBE I WANTED YOU TO FIGHT FOR ME

I wanted you to fight a little harder for me.

I wanted you to tell me that you didn't want me to go, that you would try harder, that you would find a solution. I wanted you to tell me that I was worth the risk, I was worth the chase. I wanted you to tell me that you'd rather live with me than without me.

I wanted you to hold on instead of letting go.

But you didn't. You didn't even try to stop me when I was leaving, you didn't try to say goodbye, you didn't even ask me if I truly wanted to leave or if I was just acting out of anger.

I walked away and you didn't follow me, you didn't ask me for one more chance and you didn't ask me if I would be okay without you.

I then realized that you never really fought for me in the beginning to fight for me in the end.

Everything was your way, at your convenience, when you had the time—nothing required an effort from you and everything was my fault.

I trained you that it was normal for me to please you and not ask for anything in return and I trained you that I'll never ask for more.

But I'm the girl who will always want more. I'm the girl who will never settle.

Maybe you wanted more and maybe you didn't, but either way, you never fought for more, you never asked for more and you never wanted me more.

And I know you said that fighting shouldn't be part of love, that you shouldn't fight for people who exit your life, but sometimes you have to fight for people to *stay* in your life. You must give them a reason to stay.

And I wanted you to give me a reason, a sign—a hand to hold.

But you chose not to and I was going to fight for you until I realized you never wanted to be an opponent and there is no point in fighting when the battle is already *lost*.

I wanted you to fight for me but you didn't.

But thank you for not fighting for me; you taught me how to fight for myself and that was the greatest lesson I've ever learned.

IS YOUR HEART BREAKING NOW?

Do you believe me now?

After she left you. After she broke your heart.

Do you believe me now?

When I told you I would never hurt you. When I told you I would always stay.

When I told you that I would never let anything stand in our way; not the distance, not your family, not your friends, not even my own fears and insecurities.

Do you see it now?

Or do you still need more proof? Maybe more heartbreaks? Maybe more people incapable of truly loving you?

Do you still need time to think about it? Time to figure it out? Time to see the obvious?

That maybe I'm the one and maybe you shouldn't have let me go.

Do you believe me now?

When I joked one day and told you that you'll roam the world and you won't find anything like my love. When I told you that I can't wait for you forever and maybe one of these days I'll be gone.

Do you feel it now?

The pain. The agony. The torture of loving someone who's not even yours. Of wanting someone who doesn't want you. Of waiting for something that may never happen.

Do you get it now?

How you made me feel all along. How you broke my heart. How hard it was to move on.

Do you miss me now?

TO THE LONELY NIGHTS

You seem to have enjoyed your free stay with me.

No one stayed with me as long as you stayed. No one lingered the way you did.

You're the only constant in my life. You're always here when I need you. You don't want to let me go.

But the truth is I'm tired of you. I'm sick of you. I can't wait to get rid of you.

Your silence is insipid. Your emptiness is draining. Your darkness is terrifying.

Your presence is no longer wanted. Your lessons are all learned.

I miss having people around me. I miss being surrounded by laughter and light. I miss going to bed next to someone. I miss waking up to the birds chirping and singing. I miss feeling like I coexist; I need to know that I'm not all by myself in this world.

I want you to let me go. I want you to set me free. I want you to release me from the seclusion you trapped me in.

Because I don't deserve you. I'm full of life. I'm full of love and you're sucking it all out of me.

I need you to leave me alone.

You had your time and now your time is up.

Now, I need to leave you. Now, you need to give me space. Now, you need to give up on me.

I'm breaking up with you.

You and I are done forever.

I'm leaving you to find the world.

I'm done staying up late with you thinking about what we're missing out on.

I'm going to go out there and live.

And you can have the bed all to yourself. I know I'll sleep better without you.

I know I don't want to share my bed with you anymore.

To The Ones Who Loved Us and The Ones Who Healed Us

TO THE ONE FATE BROUGHT BACK TO ME

It's easy to think that some stories have ended, to think that they will never be reopened because they already expired, only to find fate slowly bringing these stories back to your life asking for a sequel, asking for a different ending or maybe asking for a *new beginning.*

Because unlike novels, the story of our lives is written by the hands of God and only he can decide which stories end and which stories simply needed an intermission.

And just like that, he brings old people back to your life so you can start over; he brings a lover back into your life because you're both different people now and maybe this time a happy ending makes sense, maybe this time the ending doesn't have to be heartbreaking.

Maybe this time God is rooting for us.

Maybe this time you're right for me.

Because God brought you other love stories that didn't last and brought me other love stories that didn't mean anything and then he decided to bring us both back in the same place under the realm of coincidence.

And I never believed in coincidences; I believe in fate connecting two people who desperately needed to reunite for an unknown reason or maybe *forever.*

And maybe our story will end again but at least for now fate believes in you, too. It believes in *us*.

And maybe our story will end again but this time we can try to write a better one, a more loving one. A *tender* one. Maybe this time it doesn't have to end in a stalemate.

But we owe it to ourselves to at least *try*. We owe it to ourselves to respond to fate. We owe it to ourselves to listen to a universe that keeps pulling us closer together.

Because if fate brought you back to me, it means we're destined to be together, at least for a moment—*at least for now*.

And maybe forever is not our fate but I am sure it will lead us to it.

And maybe our ending is not a happy one but the beginning looks promising.

And maybe this time we should just call it love instead of calling it fate.

YOU MAKE ME WANT TO BREAK ALL THE RULES

You make me want to text you first and not think twice about what I want to say.

You make want to tell you I miss you even if we were just together the night before.

You make me want to forget that my heart was ever broken and love like I've never been hurt.

You make me want to drive to your house just to see you for two minutes.

You make me want to learn how to make all your favorite meals so I can cook them for you.

You make me want to forget about everyone I talked to before I met you.

You make me want to delete all their numbers because they don't matter anymore.

You make me want to tell my mom about you because she's been praying I'd find someone like you.

You make me want to thank God each and every night because he finally answered my prayers.

You make me want to be honest—unafraid of my feelings.

You make me want to fall in love all over again.

You make me want to work on myself and be a better person.

You make me want to wake up every morning and fall in love with life again.

You make me want to write happy poems.

You make me want to let go of everything that's been holding me back from feeling and just *feel* everything.

You make me want to stop running from everything and stay by your side.

You make me want to trust my heart again because it found you and somehow that was the best thing that ever happened to it.

You make me want to believe in fairy tales again.

You make me want to believe in miracles again.

You make me want to break all the rules and follow you.

I KNOW ENOUGH TO KNOW THAT I LIKE YOU

I don't know your favorite movie but I know I want to watch it with you on Sunday night.

I don't know your favorite restaurant but I know I want to go there with you, sipping wine, talking about our past, our adventures, our families, and our friends. I want us to exchange the deepest and most intimate stories.

I don't know your favorite country but I know I want to go there with you so we can explore its culture and its beauty as we explore the beauty within ourselves. I want us to try and understand our chaos as we walk through the chaotic streets holding hands. I want us to tour all the museums and get lost in their art. I want us to get lost in our art, too—the strokes of our own beauty and the tapestry of our own pain.

I don't know your best friends but I know I want to meet them and listen to their stories about you and your memories together. I want to see how much they love you and what kind of influence you have on them. I want to know what kind of friend you are because you will be my best friend, too.

I don't know your favorite book but I know I want to read it. I want to understand what inspires you, what moves you and the words that touch your beautiful soul. I want to know what excites your mind and what captures your heart. I want to read between the lines and decode what each sentence means to you.

I don't know if you prefer running or lifting weights but I know I want to run with you wherever you want to go and I know I want to lift some of the weight off your shoulders if you would let me. *I want to show you that you don't have to run or lift alone anymore. That the weight doesn't have to be so heavy anymore.*

I don't know who you loved before and how they loved you but I know it wasn't right. I know it left you wounded, I know it left you bleeding and I know that I may not be able to stop all the bleeding but I can make you smile again, I can make you believe again and I can try to sterilize the oldest of wounds and the deepest of cuts.

I don't know much about you but I know a lot about me. I know when my eyes see something that makes them sparkle and when my heart feels something real. I know when my hands touch something precious and when my soul connects with something *divine.*

I don't know much about you but I know enough about love and this looks a lot like love or maybe it's not but I want to find out.

I know enough to know that I want to delve deeper into your soul and scoop out the hidden gems. I know enough to know that somewhere in your depth, *I'll find my treasure.*

TO MY FAVORITE SURPRISE

It was a long Wednesday evening. I had a horrible day at work and I was drained. I looked up and asked God for something. A miracle. Magic. Anything to make me survive the miseries of the day.

On most days, God doesn't listen to me. He doesn't send me angels. He doesn't send me miracles. But some days, he surprises me. He sends me exactly what I'm asking for or something better, as if he's trying to tell me don't ever lose faith in me. I'll always show up when you desperately need me to.

And so that night I saw you.

I remember at first you didn't pay much attention to me because you were so busy being the charismatic social butterfly that you are, entertaining everyone, taking care of your friends and occasionally flirting with the pretty women in the room. Then you slowly approached me and started asking me questions I normally wouldn't answer but somehow, I answered you. *Somehow, I felt like I could tell you anything.*

We talked about work and family. We talked about what we're passionate about and our dreams. We talked about traveling and where we belong. We talked about everything but we didn't talk about love.

Maybe we didn't want to know too much. Maybe we already secretly knew. Maybe we didn't want to make it awkward but we talked all night and miraculously I forgot about my day, my work and my troubles. Somehow looking at you made me feel like there's nothing that look couldn't fix. There's nothing that look couldn't heal. There's nothing that look couldn't take away.

Because it took my breath away and it took my heart away.

Even though I knew you were not innocent, the way you looked at me was. It wasn't the look you give other girls to sweep them off their feet. It was different. It was *respectful.*

And the problem is every time you see something real, you don't know what to do. Every time you think this could be love, you back off. You run away. You try so hard not to fall.

And I knew that but I wasn't as strong as you were. *I fell.* I still fall every time I see you.

Maybe you're not my forever. But that day I asked for a miracle. I asked for magic. And I saw you.

Maybe you're not my happy ending. But you'll always be my *magic.*

You'll always be the one who saved the day.

TO GIORGOS: THE GREEK RESTAURANT OWNER
WHO WANTED TO PROPOSE TO ME

I went to Greece with my friends last summer and while we were all drunk on the beautiful scenery and the sublime views of the mountains in Santorini, I was also drunk from all the Greek wine we've been drinking all day and when I'm wine-drunk, I like to start deep conversations with strangers. I find it really refreshing to talk to someone who doesn't know a thing about me, someone who probably won't see me again. I like talking to strangers about the trials and tribulations of my life and maybe even confide in them a little bit more than I should.

That's when I met Giorgos, the owner of a cute little authentic Greek restaurant in Oia. I was asking Giorgos about the beautiful Greek culture and how many love stories and proposals he witnesses a day, given that he lives in one of the most romantic cities on Earth. He went on to tell me stories that literally brought tears to my eyes and reawakened my faith in humanity and romance.

After listening to his beautiful stories in his endearing Greek accent, I opened up to him about the guy I was into and how little of an effort he's been making with me. I told him that I think it's because he's scared of being with me and breaking my heart because we have a lot of common friends. He knows that if he messes things up, he might not be able to recover from it.

Poor Giorgos looked at me like I was coming from another planet. He then told me something that stuck with me to this day. He said, *"You know how many proposals I witness a day? At least 10. Most of these men are terrified the girl might say no but they bend down on one knee anyway because they're holding on to the possibility of her saying 'yes.' The yes that will change their lives. That yes that will make their dreams come true."*

Then he said, "This boy knows you will say yes and he still doesn't want to even try." Then he joked and said "Make him jealous and tell him a very sexy, rich and handsome Greek man proposed to me in Santorini and he will make me happy. I will marry you today if you say yes." I laughed out loud at how charming and funny Giorgos was but after my conversation with him, I walked by myself for a few minutes to take in the heavenly beauty of Santorini at night but I couldn't get his words out of my head.

Men propose and they're not sure the girl will say yes, but their profound love for their women makes them fearless, it makes them run the risk of shattering their hearts into a million pieces and here I am thinking that the boy is not texting me because he's scared of hurting me. Sometimes I surprise myself by how lame and pathetic I can be when I like someone!

I then thought of taking Giorgos's advice and tell him that a handsome Greek man proposed to me, but then I asked myself if he'll even care or if it will even matter to him.

And I guess that's all I needed. A reminder that I deserve someone who wants to at least try even if I might say no. A reminder that a stranger in Greece told me that he'd propose to me and the boy I wanted to give my heart to didn't even want to date me.

And maybe we all need a 'Giorgos' in our lives to remind us of our worth and tell us not to settle and maybe we should all be looking for that person who thinks our 'yes' will change their life—the person who thinks we're their dream.

WILL YOU BE MINE?

I remember when you asked me these words and I looked at you in utter disbelief because you never showed me a sign, you never told me you liked me, you never looked at me the way others look at me and you never said anything more than hello.

And then one night you asked me if I wanted to be yours and I said no because I didn't even know you; I was too busy getting to know the ones who tried harder. The ones who said all the right things and swept me off my feet.

But later, I realized that it's the ones who are silently watching, it's the ones who are observing from afar, it's the ones who don't say much that actually care the most.

They're the ones who know your intricacies, they're the ones who hold the deepest love in their hearts for you. They're the ones who think about you day and night, waiting for the moment they muster up enough courage to come and tell you how they really feel.

And I realized that the ones who talk, the ones who charm you, the ones who act like they want you more than anyone are the ones who pretend. They tell everyone what they want to hear. They enjoy playing this game and winning. They're the ones who want validation from as many people as possible. They're the ones who look at you as a challenge rather than a piece of art.

And you saw me as art.

And I wish I had said yes.

I wish you and I made art.

I wish you and I crafted a *masterpiece.*

I KNOW WE'RE FRIENDS
BUT I THINK YOU'RE CUTE

I know we're friends but sometimes I like the way you smile a little too much.

I know we're friends but sometimes I like it when you dance with me, a lot more than I should.

I know we're friends but sometimes I think of what would happen if we were more.

I know we're friends but I like the way you look at me when you think I'm not looking.

I know we're friends but sometimes I dream about you.

I know we're friends but I love seeing your name on my phone.

I know we're friends and I know we're better off as friends.

I know we're both afraid of losing each other and we're scared to try.

I know we're friends but sometimes I wonder if our friendship is a blessing or a curse.

I know we're friends but sometimes I wish we weren't; sometimes I wish we didn't have so much to lose.

I know we're friends but sometimes I think maybe we could fall in love.

TO THE ONE WHO WILL ALWAYS LOVE ME

You taught me that when it comes to love, I shouldn't settle.

You taught me that those who love me will never stop trying, they will never stop coming back and they will never hold back their feelings.

You taught me that those who truly love me will not give up easily, they'll keep fighting, they'll keep showing up and they'll be there for me time and time again.

But more than anything, you taught me that those who truly love me will never stop. Those who truly care don't just disappear, they don't just move on and they don't act like I meant nothing to them.

You taught me that I'll always be enough for the ones who care.

You taught me that I'll always be loved no matter how far I go.

You taught me that love doesn't really end. It doesn't really go away. It's not easily replaced.

Maybe you were meant to love me so you can teach me more about love.

Maybe you were meant to love me so you can show me that it's okay to love others even if they don't love you back.

Maybe you're a symbol of the love I want even though you're not the one.

I guess love is not something that can be tamed, it's not something that can be measured.

I guess love is not something you can really calculate.

It's also not something you can shape. Love is not something you can box.

And maybe that's why it's so crazy and it doesn't make sense that you still love me and I still can't get myself to love you back.

And it's crazy that I'm waiting to find someone I can love the way you love me.

I hope I can find someone I'll never stop loving. The way you never stopped loving me.

TO THE ONE WHO FEELS LIKE A DREAM

I had a dream about you.

You were close.

You said you loved me.

You said you cared.

You asked me about my future.

You asked me about my past.

You asked me about my family.

You asked me about my friends.

You asked me about my work.

You asked me about my ex.

You asked me everything.

And I told you everything.

And you understood.

You didn't flinch.

You weren't scared.

You were brave.

It was a long dream.

It's the dream I dream every day.

It's the dream I dream when I'm wide awake.

It's the dream that always involves you.

It's the dream that I don't want to wake up from.

Unless you're the one waking me up.

I'LL ALWAYS ANSWER YOUR CALL

I'll always be one call away. If you need a friend to talk to. If you need someone to listen to you and understand you.

If you need to take a trip down memory lane and remember all the times we had together; the funny moments we shared, the crazy memories and the nights we stayed up talking and watching the sunrise.

I'll always be one plane ticket away. If you're in trouble, if you need someone by your side, if you need someone to hold your hand, you can always count on me. I'll always be there for you. No matter how long it's been or how far you are.

I'll always be near. I'll always find you.

I'll always be there for you; all you have to do is *ask*.

I'll always be there to remind you that you're not alone. I'm here. I've always been here. I'll always be here.

And I know we both moved on and I know we don't always stay in touch or say what's in our hearts but I hope you know that even if I don't say much, even if I don't show it, I'll always be close to you. I'll always care about you. I'll always want to help you when you need someone.

You were always good at hearing my silence; you were always good at understanding me without saying a word and I hope this time is no different. I hope you understand that even when I'm quiet, I can still hear you.

I'll always be one call away. If you need to talk for hours or if you need to remember that you are loved. I'll always be there to let you know just how loved and how incredible you are.

I'll always remind you that you're unforgettable and that you're not alone.

IN A WORLD TRYING TO MAKE YOU FEEL ALONE, I'LL ALWAYS BE BY YOUR SIDE

In a world trying to make you feel ugly, I'll always show you your beauty; the beauty that lies within, the beauty that only a few people can show you, the beauty that you sometimes forget you have because of all the things people told you and all the lies they made you believe.

In a world trying to make you feel like a failure, I'll remind you of your accomplishments, I'll remind you of the days you fought so hard to be where you are today. I'll remind you of the nights you couldn't stop crying but eventually found a way to smile again and I'll remind you of how far you've come, how strong you're becoming and how resilient you really are.

In a world trying to make you feel unloved, I'll love you with all my heart. I'll love you when you're moody. I'll love you when you're weak. I'll love you when you're quiet. I'll love you when you're scared. I'll love you when you're lost and I'll love you when you can't name one thing you love about yourself. I'll write you a list of everything I love about you. I'll see the things that no one sees. I'll introduce you to a new kind of love. A love you never thought existed. *The kind of love you deserve.*

In a world trying to make you believe that everyone is shady, I'll be the one thing that's real. I'll be kind. I'll be genuine. I won't take you for granted. I won't only love you when you're happy or rich or successful. I won't walk out on you when you're at your lowest. I'll always fight for you. I'll always stand by you. I'll always be on your side. We'll always be on the same team, whether we win or lose. *I'll always root for you.*

In a world trying to convince you that everyone is going to betray you, I'll prove to you my loyalty time and time again. I'll make you *trust* again. I'll make you believe that people can stay.

I'll make you realize that history doesn't always have to repeat itself. I'll make you realize that some risks are still worth taking and some chances can change your life. I'll remind you that if you take a leap of faith, you can change your whole world. A world that makes you feel beautiful. A world that makes you feel safe. A world where you don't have to worry about being alone because I'll always be right beside you.

HE WAS MY STORM BUT YOU'RE MY CALM

You get mad when I talk about him. You get quiet when people say his name.

You think he's still a threat. You think he's the one that got away.

And I won't lie and say he wasn't, because for the longest time, he was the one that got away. The one I was almost certain I'd end up with eventually.

But then you came along and you showed me that stars still shine in the darkest of nights. You showed me that the sun doesn't always have to burn. You showed me that we don't have to run and hide when it rains. You showed me how beautiful the moon is when you have the right person by your side.

You showed me that I could be loved just the way I am. You showed me that I could be me and still make your heart skip a beat. Because you don't ask me to laugh quietly, you love how loud my laugh is. You don't ask me to stop eating because this is my fifth meal. You don't ask me to stop being so emotional or so sensitive because you know that this is my heart and you love it the way it is.

He always had something to say. He always disliked something. He always made me feel insecure about the things

I should be proud of. He always made me feel like he's doing me a favor by being with me.

He started a storm within me, a storm that I thought he was the only one who could stop.

But then you came along and you made me realize that the person who caused the storm should be forgotten in it, the person who caused the storm will not be the one to rescue me from it.

But you're the calm. You're the rainbow after the hurricane. You're the rise after the fall.

You always have something beautiful to say, something fascinating, something endearing, something sincere, something mesmerizing and something lovable.

So he may be the one that got away, but whoever said that the one that got away needs to come back? Sometimes the one that got away is better away. Sometimes he must go away to make room for someone better to come along.

Sometimes he's the chaos that leaves so the calm can stay.

TO MY FAVORITE ACCIDENT

I met you when I wasn't looking, I bumped into you when I was looking for someone else. I met you when I was still trying to pick up the pieces. But as soon as I met you, I knew that something about you was going to change something about me. I knew from the moment we said hello that we won't be saying goodbye anytime soon.

Isn't it funny how our hearts just give us cues about certain people? How they decide to swiftly unlock themselves from their own chains and open up to someone they just met?

And from the very first day you unlocked my heart, from the very first day I knew my heart wanted you.

Maybe accidents aren't really accidents; maybe these coincidences are strategically planned so that two people can find each other when they were desperately searching for one another, or maybe they're planned so that two people can find each other when they were desperately searching for someone else.

Maybe they serve as a reminder that someone out there is so much better for us, someone out there is exactly who we need to forget about the ones who took us for granted and the ones who broke our hearts.

Sometimes I wonder if I'm just fantasizing because the hopeless romantic in me always takes over, but then no fantasy can feel so real, no fantasy can move my heart the way you do and no fantasy can be so tangible, so perceptible and so solid.

I don't know where the road may take us but I'm enjoying the ride.

I don't know where you're taking me but I know I trust you to lead the way, I trust you to take me to all the places that you love and all the places that you used to drive to alone.

And even though I suck at hiking, I'm ready to climb a mountain with you, I'm ready to be on top of the world with you.

I met you when I wasn't looking, I bumped into you when I was looking for someone else, but I found you and you turned out to be better than anyone I was looking for.

I REALIZED THAT MY LIFE IS
WHEREVER YOU ARE

Life is wherever you're near. Life is wherever I can see you and talk to you. Life is wherever I know I can come over when I'm lonely and hold your hand when I'm scared.

Life is wherever you're with me. Because it's easier to handle the downfalls, it's easier to fall knowing you're there to catch me and it's easier to live another day knowing you will be there.

Life is wherever you take me. As long as I'm with you, I know I'm safe. As long as I'm with you, I know I don't have to wonder about anything and as long as I'm with you, *life makes sense.*

Because I've been to the most beautiful places and I've seen the most beautiful faces and I still felt alone without you.

I felt dead inside; it was killing me to see the world when you weren't there, it was killing me to share the best moments in my life with someone else.

I realized that life is not about what you see but more about who you see it with.

And I'm meant to see life with you, I'm meant to live next to you because otherwise I'm not really living when I'm missing you.

People told me I can go wherever I can go and be whoever I can be and I still choose to be next to you and choose to be yours.

Because the world is huge but without you it feels so small. The world is wonderful but without you it's lifeless.

Life is wherever you are because you know how to bring me back to life.

Life is wherever you're close because a moment with you is worth more than a thousand moments with someone else.

Life is hard but with you it's easier.

Life is frustrating but with you it's delightful.

Life means nothing if you're not in it.

A SINCERE LETTER TO ALL THE ONES
I LEFT BACK HOME

It's been a hard journey but I'm finally heading some-where. The road is still long and the destination is not crystal clear but I've finally learned how to drive in the fog and keep on driving until the sun shines again.

I sometimes wish I could just go back home and not have to deal with any of these hurdles, but I feel like some-thing big is waiting for me at the end of the road. I need to go find myself away from the comfort of my own bed and the sound of your lullabies.

I had to leave so I can grow, so I can be the person you told me I could be, so I can reach the potential you saw in me that I couldn't see in myself and the person you wanted me to be.

I have tried to find people like you to make the road easier but it was hard to find anyone that could replace you be-cause you're irreplaceable and it would be unfair to com-pare anyone I meet to you. No one will do our friendship and our bond justice. You are the blessings that come only once in a lifetime.

I realized there's so much more to explore outside the can-opy of our little jokes and conversations, outside the luxury of not having to explain ourselves to anyone or wonder if someone misunderstood us and outside the silence we never really feared, but here silence makes you think, it makes you question, it could drive you crazy.

Here, silence is terrifying.

I thought about coming home. I thought about going back again because it's easier.

But I didn't want to come home the same person that left and I didn't want to come home without a fight, I didn't want to come home when I haven't battled anyone. I wanted to come back as a winner, a champion or a fighter, someone who fought till the end, someone who tried and someone who didn't let you down.

But I want you to know that you keep me going more than anyone. Whenever I feel hopeless, I remember the nights we strolled in the city laughing, singing our lungs out as we walked arm in arm. I remember the nights we held each other tightly whenever one of us was hurting and I remember all the crazy memories we had and the silly things we did and these memories make me feel *alive.* They make me smile when I'm tired. They make me look forward to the day I come back to you.

They remind me of how lucky I am that I have people like you to come home to. They remind me that no matter how far I wander, you're still close to me, closer than ever.

And I want you to know that I will be okay. At times, I may get lost and I may struggle to stay in touch with you but I will never completely disappear. I will never be distant. I will never change with you.

I want you to know that I didn't leave because of you; I left because of me.

Because of the person I was becoming, the person I was turning into and because I started to feel like I didn't belong. But throughout this journey, I learned that home doesn't have to be one place, that you could have many homes in your lifetime but you'll still have one special home you loved more, one special home you miss, one special home you had the best time in.

But I want you to know that wherever my final home will be, miles and miles away or a block away, I will always love you and you will forever be my favorite home. You will always be the reason why I will keep on fighting and why I will try to win.

You will always be in my heart.

You will always be irreplaceable.

You will always be the home I'll never forget.

To The
Ones Who
Made Us
Ask
Important
Questions

And The
Ones Who
Gave Us
The
Answers

I DON'T KNOW WHAT TO TELL MY MOM ABOUT YOU ANYMORE

My mom asked me about you today...*again*!

I'm running out of excuses to tell her. I'm running out of lies.

She asked me if you're coming to my aunt's gathering and I told her you're busy.

She asked me if you're coming to my cousin's wedding and I told her your parents are in town.

She asked me if you're coming to my best friend's birthday and I told her you have an important meeting at work.

She asked me if you're taking that road trip with me and I told her you couldn't take any days off.

I know that eventually, my mom will stop asking me about you because she's starting to realize that maybe we're *nothing*.

She's going to think you're just another one of my fantasies, another one of my romantic illusions. Another love I imagined.

And I can't blame her.

I always told her about people she never met, people who

never cared to see her, people who didn't try to make her feel that her daughter is in safe hands.

But I told her about you because I thought you were different. I thought this was *it*.

And maybe I shouldn't have told her anything about you, because when I asked you what we were, you said 'I don't know' and I guess that means that I know what we're *not*.

We're not together.

You're not mine.

Next time my mom asks me about you, I'll use your answer: I'll tell her I don't know.

And you'll remain another name on her list—another stranger that came into her daughter's life then broke her heart. A name she may never remember or never forget.

I'M TIRED OF LYING TO PEOPLE ABOUT YOU

I'm tired of telling them that you're always busy because you're ambitious and you're focused on your career.

I'm tired of telling them that you didn't leave because you didn't love me; you just left so you can work on yourself.

I'm tired of telling them that you care. I'm tired of trying to convince everyone, including myself, that you genuinely care.

I'm also tired of lying to myself.

I'm tired of sugarcoating the truth so I can keep you in my life.

I'm tired of telling my friends that you're into me so they can stop telling me to move on.

I'm tired of not following my own advice.

I'm tired of pretending that you didn't break my heart and that I'm not expecting anything more.

I'm tired of waiting for you.

I'm tired of believing you.

I'm tired of loving you.

I'm tired of lying to people and telling them that you love me, too.

ALL THE QUESTIONS I WANTED TO ASK YOU
BUT I ASKED 'HOW'S WORK?' INSTEAD

Do you miss me?
(because I do)

Are you happy?
(because I'm not)

Are you wondering why I've been so distant?
(because you hurt me)

Do you know why and you just don't care?
(because that would hurt so much more)

Do you still care?
(because I still do)

Was it all an act? Was it all a game?
(because it was real for me)

Did you move on?
(because I can't let go)

Do you love someone else?
(because I can love you better)

Do you think I'm crazy?
(because you're driving me crazy)

Are you scared?
(because I'm terrified)

Why did you disappear?
(because I still don't understand)

Do you want to ask me anything?
(because I'll tell you everything)

Do you think we still have a chance?
(because that's all I ever wanted)

PERHAPS ALL I NEEDED WAS AN ANSWER

Perhaps all I needed was an answer instead of you calling me cold.

I turned cold when your warmth got icy. I turned cold when your words turned flat. I turned cold because you left without a word. You didn't give me an answer. A reason. An excuse. You didn't say anything.

Perhaps all I needed was an answer instead of pretending like I never existed.

Maybe I needed a proper goodbye, I needed something more to prove to me that you at least enjoyed our moments and appreciated the time we spent together. All I needed was a text to let me know that even though it didn't last, it was special.

All I needed was something from you to let me know that it was real. That we were both on the same page. That for a moment, we were one.

Perhaps all I needed was an answer instead of leaving me alone with all my thoughts.

And you know how much I overthink and you know how much it kills me when people leave without saying a word and you know how my thoughts keep me up at night. You know that I tend to be too hard on myself. You know that

I'm going to think it was me. That I pushed you away. That it was my fault. I wish you made it a little bit easier to love myself even if you couldn't love me.

Perhaps I already have the answer—it's just not what I wanted to hear.

Perhaps your silence is the answer. Perhaps your departure is the answer. Perhaps acting like you don't care is not an act and you really don't. Perhaps I'm waiting for you to be someone you'll never be. Perhaps honesty and courage are not qualities you possess.

Perhaps all you know how to be is a *coward*.

ALL I NEEDED WAS ONE COFFEE DATE

I wasn't asking for too much.

I wasn't asking for red roses and romantic dates.

I wasn't asking for a trip to Paris or Rome.

All I wanted was one coffee date for you to see another side of me.

The side that listens more than speaks, the side that asks the right questions, the side that doesn't try to be loud or funny or crazy, the side that comes out when the world is still, when the world is still and my mind is quiet.

I wanted you to see that underneath the fun and bubbly girl there's a layer of depth, a layer of serenity, a layer of wisdom and a layer of empathy caused by the pain and the suffering my heart endured.

I wanted you to see how I could've understood you and your story.

I wanted you to see that our communication could have been effortless.

I wanted you to see that I wasn't going to judge you for your past mistakes.

I guess I thought I could show you that side one day over coffee. I guess I thought you would at least ask me out for coffee.

But I never had the chance; you assumed that I'm someone else and that we're not a good fit.

You assumed that we're destined to fall apart before you even try.

But I didn't want to think about the future, I didn't want to think about our differences, I just wanted to grab coffee with you, to see you in the daytime, to talk to you when you're sober, to show you a side few people have seen.

I guess you never thought about it as much as I did.

Or maybe you don't like coffee or maybe you just don't like me.

All I needed was one coffee date so I could truly move on because now I see you and I think about that coffee date and what would have happened if we had met up for coffee that day and how it could have changed our lives—or at least mine.

But for now, I'll drink coffee alone at a coffee shop and wait for the one who wants to drink coffee with me, probe all my sides, talk about his life and mine, ask deep and silly questions, laugh and cry, and maybe—just maybe— fall in love with me.

I FINALLY LEARNED WHAT TO DO
WHEN I MISS YOU

I'll find your texts to read the emptiness in your words, to remember how your actions never matched your words. I'll find them so I can read the broken promises over and over again and remember that you not only broke your promises; you also broke my heart.

I'll check your profile to see how many women you're flirting with to remember that you never thought I was special, how many admirers you have and all the pretty girls that give you the attention you desire. I'll remember how you never stopped playing your games after you met me. I want to remember how your eyes and your mind were never set on me. I want to see all the evidence that proves that you never really cared—even if it hurts.

I'll remember that you don't miss me, too. I'll remember that you haven't tried to reach out or say a word. I'll feel your absence and I'll remember that I needed more. I'll remember that you failed to give me what I wanted.

I don't know why when people leave, we assume that it's our fault, that there's something wrong with us but sometimes it's their fault, they couldn't give us what we're looking for either, they didn't understand our needs and they couldn't grasp how we want to be loved or provide us with the kind of love we deserve.

It's not a crime to want more and I wanted more. Much more than what you were giving me.

You thought I'd be okay with poor communication and inconsistency. You thought I'd be okay with being just another one of your girls. You thought I'd be okay with waiting for you and pretending like I don't want more. You thought I'll continue being your friend until you decide.

But you should have known better. You should have known that when I tell you I like you, it means I *only* like you because that's not something that happens very often. I don't usually fall for a bunch of men at the same time. I don't know how to make them all feel special and cared for.

I don't know how to give them just enough to string them along. I'm not you.

I don't give in easily but when I do, I give my all. I don't fall often but when I do, I fall too hard.

And I thought you'd know that because of how well you were able to analyze me, but I should have known better. I should have known that no matter what you see in me, you'll never *appreciate* it.

So that's what I'll do when I start missing you. I'll remember that you missed out on me and it was your *choice*. I'll remember that you weren't looking for love. I'll remember that you weren't looking for *me*.

I'll keep remembering everything until I stop missing you. Until I forget you.

THIS IS ME ACCEPTING THAT THINGS WILL NEVER BE THE SAME BETWEEN US

This is me accepting that we'll still be in each other's lives but not necessarily involved in them. We'll see each other and make small talk but we won't share the details we used to share or trust each other with our deepest secrets or ask each other for advice.

This is me accepting that we'll forgive each other but we'll never forget. There will always be this cloud hovering over us when we talk, there will always be this memory of the night things changed and there will always be this voice inside our heads reminding us of the words we said that we can't take back.

This is me accepting that you won't be there for every occasion, every milestone, every high and every low. This is me getting used to your absence, getting used to celebrating life without you. This is me getting used to depending on anyone other than you.

This is me accepting that you won't be the first person I call when things go wrong. You won't be the person who will protect me or make me feel safe. This is me getting used to fighting alone. This is me getting used to walking alone at night without waiting for you to lead the way.

This is me accepting that life will go on without you, it

will still make sense, it will still have meaning and it will still be beautiful. This is me getting used to finding pleasure in the simple things and making new memories. This is me tearing the perfect picture I had in mind for us— this is me taking new pictures without you in them.

This is me accepting that our connection will always be disconnected, our love will always be broken and our bond will always be frail. This is me getting used to being alone. This is me learning how to find my own worth away from you. This is me acknowledging that I'll always be enough for me even if I wasn't enough for you.

IF THEY EVER ASK YOU WHY SHE CHANGED

Tell them she gave me her heart
and I threw it away.
Tell them she waited for me,
time and time again
but I never showed up.

Tell them all she wanted to do
was love me
and all I did was let her go.
Tell them she declared her love
to the whole world
but I never told a soul.

Tell them she wanted to ease my loneliness,
she wanted to make the night less terrifying
and all I did was leave her alone at night,
in her bed *crying*.

Tell them she gave me more than one chance
but I ruined them all.
Tell them she listened to all my stories
but I never asked her about one of her chapters.

Tell them she changed because I made her,
because every time she'd get closer
I'd find ways to push her away
and every time she tried to love me,
I made her love herself a little less.

Tell them she changed because
she was the only one caring,
she was the only one loving
and she was only one *hurting*.

Tell them she changed because she finally realized
that I'll never give her what she wants
and she finally realized that she deserves someone
who gives her everything she wants and *more*.

I'M SORRY YOU HAD TO PAY FOR HIS MISTAKE

You both come from the same city. You both have the same charm. You both have the same zodiac sign. You both have the same enthralling gaze. You're both irresistible. You both captured my heart.

But he broke my heart *twice.*

He made me so happy then made me so miserable.

It took me years to get over him. It took me years to get over what he did. It took me years to forget the way he made me feel.

And then I met you. And you mesmerized me because that's what you do. You hypnotize people.

You were better than him. He was cruel. You seemed kind. The way he looked at me wasn't real but with you, I felt something. I liked the way you looked at me. I liked the way you admired me.

So, I surrendered.

Even though I promised myself that I will be guarded with guys like you, I still wanted to get to know you. I still wanted to know if I'll ever have a chance with guys like you.

But then you started acting like him. Your responses got shorter, your eyes didn't look at me with the same fervor, your mind was somewhere else and I was hoping that your heart was still with me. I was hoping that there was still hope and I tried not to kill it with my insecurities or my fears. And I tried not to compare you to him.

I let you go but I sent it out to the universe that I still want you. I needed a sign. I needed a message from the universe, and because the universe gives you the answers you desperately need, the inevitable happened.

The universe gave me the sign I needed. I saw you with her. I saw you kissing her. I saw you leave with her.

And I hated you for it. Maybe hate is a strong word but you made me remember him and what he did to me. I had to relive the pain of losing him all over again on top of the pain of losing you. You brought with you the ghosts of the past and the present. *The ghosts of heartbreak.*

The problem with heartbreak is that it triggers certain memories, certain emotions, certain fears and suddenly you're not yourself.

Suddenly you act like a completely different person to protect yourself. Suddenly, you're hostile.

And I wanted to protect myself from you.

And maybe you're not exactly like him, but you both didn't really want me as much as I wanted you. You were both selfish. You both didn't care about my feelings.

I'm sorry you had to pay for his mistake.

I'm sorry I saw him in you.

I'm sorry I ran away without telling you why.

But now I know why they warned me. Now I know why they told me to stay away from guys like you. Now I know why you two have a lot more in common than I thought.

Now I know why you both broke my heart.

It's ironic though because now I see him and I don't feel a thing but I still avoid him because now he reminds me of you.

I CAN'T SEE YOU AND PRETEND LIKE NOTHING HAPPENED

Maybe that's my problem. Maybe I'm just too sensitive. Maybe I just can't forget or maybe you were just that important. Maybe I wanted a lot more than this. A lot more than just small talk.

But I just can't see you and pretend like we're normal. I can't see you and pretend like it's all good.

I can't see you and pretend that you didn't hurt me.

I can't see you and not think about all the things I wanted to talk to you about instead of talking about work and the weather. All the secrets I wanted to share with you and all the stories I wish you had told me. I can't see you and pretend like I don't wonder what could have been or why you had to disappear.

I can't pretend like I don't know about her. I can't pretend like I don't know you're giving her your attention, your time and your love. I can't pretend like it doesn't bother me every time I see you and remember that you picked her and I still don't understand why.

I can't get over how quickly things ended, how quickly they *collapsed*. I can't get over how you didn't say a word and how I didn't ask you a single question. I can't get over this silence or how quickly you replaced me. *I just can't.*

Part of me just wants to be honest with you and tell you everything, tell you that the next time you see me, pretend like you don't know me because I'm already *invisible* to you. Part of me just wants to tell you that you don't have to be nice or cordial because it all doesn't matter now. It's all the same to me.

You're not mine and until you are, there's nothing you can do that will fix it.

I can't see you and treat you like a stranger or a friend. I can't see you and pretend like I don't want to touch you or tell you that I miss you. I can't see you and pretend like it's over because to me, it's not.

To me, it didn't even start.

To me, it still doesn't make any sense. It doesn't add up. You, kissing someone else—me, loving someone else. *It just doesn't.*

YOU LEFT A LONG TIME AGO, SO
DON'T TRY TO COME BACK NOW

You left on a gloomy winter day. You left without saying goodbye. You left without telling me that you're not coming back.

You left and you made me get used to people leaving, you made me get used to being alone.

But I found myself alone in the desert, looking for water, looking for food, looking for people and looking for an exit.

You left me all by myself: lost, sad and confused.

You left me stranded, voiceless, trying to ask for help.

And maybe I died a few times but I found a way to live. I found myself again.

I found a way to feed my mind, to nourish my soul and use my voice again.

I found a way to stay warm and dry in the storm.

I don't know how I did it. I don't know how I survived. I don't know why I wanted to live.

I just knew that I saw the sunlight and it made me long for something brighter, something better—a life without you.

Because a life without you meant a life of freedom, a life of hope, a life of sunny days and starry nights. A life without you meant a life where I can be myself and not have to apologize for it.

I wanted to live before I die. I wanted to experience what it was like to be happy. To smile every day and laugh every night.

And I found it.

And now I'm happy.

I'm fine without you.

So you can't come back now. You're not welcome. You're not invited.

My door is now closed. You can't break me again.

That's what you get when you exit someone's life before they're ready—you don't come back whenever you're ready.

You no longer have the upper hand. You no longer have the key. I changed the locks and I changed myself.

TO THE GIRL WHO THINKS THAT
SHE MUST BE THE PROBLEM

I get it.

I've been there.

You think it must be you because he started dating someone else right after he told you he wasn't ready.

You think it must be you because it happened to you repeatedly, from different men and they can't all be that bad.

You're the one thing they all have in common.

You think it must be you because you keep pushing them away, into the arms of other women.

You think it must be you because they never resurfaced, they never came back and they never apologized for letting you go.

You think it must be you because of all the unresolved childhood issues you have, you think it's because you still have a lot of things to work on and a lot of things to fix. You think maybe you're unfixable.

You think it must be you because you want love so much and every time you try to ask for it, you get denied. Every time you think it's real, it fools you.

You think it's you because maybe on a deeper level, you stopped believing that you deserve it. Maybe on a deeper level, you don't believe that you will find it and you keep falling for those who prove you right.

I'm not going to tell you that you are perfect, that it's definitely them not you and I'm not going to tell you that you're better than them but I am going to tell you that even if you're the problem, someone who really wants you will not run away.

Someone who really wants you will try to understand where the problem is coming from; he will try to find answers, maybe a solution.

He will try to listen before he shuts off, he will try to talk to you before he stops responding to your messages, he will try to spend more time with you before he decides he doesn't want to see you anymore. He will try before he gives up. He should at least *try*.

I know you're too hard on yourself, but you also find people who are harder on you. You find people who make you feel like your problems are insoluble.

But even if you are the problem, even if you don't always say or do the right things, it shouldn't be a deal-breaker, it shouldn't be a reason for someone to stop trying. We all have problems we're still trying to solve but we don't need someone who wants us with no baggage and no problems, we don't need someone who takes the easy way out.

We need someone who helps us face our problems, helps us unload our baggage and loves even the most incomplete parts of who we are.

TO THE ONE WHO ASKED ME TO CHANGE
SO I COULD FIND LOVE

Don't ask me to stop being so emotional or too vulnerable because this sends men running the other way. Don't ask me to stop being myself for someone who can't handle all of me.

Don't ask me to start playing games because all guys love the chase, don't ask me to try to impress the ones who will leave once the game is over.

Don't make me feel bad because I got lost in a moment or because I said too much. Don't make me feel bad for being the one who cares more or the one who will always give someone a second chance.

Don't make me feel bad for believing. Believing in love, believing in people, believing in change and believing that only love can change people—only love can change the world.

Don't ask me to change for someone so they can love me more or give me a chance. Don't make me fall into the same trap that keeps this generation from finding love.

Don't ask me to participate in everything I hate about modern love, don't ask me to be like everyone else in this generation: afraid to feel, afraid to get hurt and afraid to love.

Ask me to be myself because the right person will not have a problem with it. Ask me to be myself because wearing a mask is nothing but a waste of time. Ask me to keep believing because this is half the battle.

And ask me to always love with all my heart because you never know what tomorrow may bring and it's better to live with answers than die with questions.

Because the truth is that love is supposed to change you for the better, it's supposed to enhance all the good things in you and it's supposed to fuel more love.

Love is supposed to make you feel better about yourself, it's not supposed to make you feel like everything you're doing will never appeal to someone else.

Because someone out there is looking for exactly everything I have to offer. Someone out there is also tired of people asking him to change so he could find love. Someone out there thinks I exist and he's right.

But don't tell me that I'm failing at finding love because of who I am. I'm not failing; I just haven't found love yet because I haven't met the right person yet.

I haven't found love because I don't want to change to be with the wrong person. I don't want to fool someone into loving who I am *not*.

I am waiting for the one who will love me for who I am and won't ask me to change so he can be with me.

THIS IS ME SAYING GOODBYE

This is me unbelieving all your lies. This is me realizing that I can't hold on to words you said when you were drunk and emotions you felt when you were lonely. This is me realizing that your actions never matched your words and your feelings were never real. This is me acknowledging that this whole time I was living a lie because I didn't want to lose you.

This is me losing you. This is me deleting your pictures. This is me erasing your messages. This is me forgetting your words. This is me losing our friendship and losing our love. This is me losing you and I mean it this time. This is me living without ever thinking of going back to you.

This is me making the decision I should have made a long time ago. This is me kicking you out of my heart. This is me making room for someone else. Someone better than you. Someone who knows what love is. Someone who appreciates me. Someone who is everything you're not. Someone who reminds me of the love that I deserve.

This is me finally saying goodbye. Goodbye to all the plans I had for us. Goodbye to the future I pictured you in. Goodbye to all the places I wanted to take you to and all the things I wanted to share with you. Goodbye to all the stories that I wanted to write for you. Goodbye to everything that has your name on it. Goodbye to everything that reminds me of you.

This is me loving myself. This is me finally realizing that I can't love you and love myself, too. This is me finally understanding that you were the only person blocking me from finding true love. This is me finally deciding that I'm not going to punish myself anymore by loving you. This is me letting go of all the resentment and the bitterness. This is me realizing that you are the biggest punishment to yourself.

A LETTER TO TIME AND TIMING

What is it about you and me? Why are you always a barrier in my relationships? Why are you always wrong? Why are you always in a different zone?

I'm tired of hearing *'wrong timing'* or *'the timing sucks'* or *'it's just bad timing'* yet it seems like most people out there don't have a problem with timing; it seems like people are making timing work despite the distance, the problems, the crazy ex-girlfriend or the psycho ex-boyfriend because somehow you don't meddle in their relationships, somehow you don't interfere and push one of them away.

But with me, you're always there. You're all I ever hear and even though I never believed in you, you seem to really believe in me.

Please leave when you feel like I'm getting close to someone, don't send your alarms running to warn them that they might be getting attached and they have to leave the country soon and long-distance might be hard. Let them take a chance on me, let me show them that distance doesn't have to be so hard and let them follow their heart, the way I always follow mine.

Please leave when I'm talking to someone who's still thinking about an ex; don't keep reminding them that they have unfinished business or that their ex might come back. Let them fall for me, let them give me the same chance they gave their ex—maybe I can make them forget, maybe I'll be the one to show them what they were missing.

Please leave when you see me falling for someone who's not ready, don't keep telling them that they're not and that they can't settle down. Let them be ready for me, let them change their mind, let them see how things will go if they try. Let me show them that even if they're not ready, they won't regret loving me.

Maybe if you leave, they'll be compelled to stay.

Bring me the right people at the right time, bring me the ones who are ready, the ones who are not hung up on an ex, who are not leaving the city anytime soon, who are not going to believe in you as much as the others did.

Bring me the ones who fight you, who make you right even if you're wrong, the ones who break every clock to make you align with me.

To All The
people
Who Once
Came Into
Our
Lives

and
Left an
Impact,
Left a
Mark, or
Left a
Scar

IF THIS IS THE END OF OUR STORY,
I WANT YOU TO KNOW THAT YOU'RE
MY FAVORITE CHAPTER

I don't believe that timing should be a barrier in moving a relationship forward. Maybe it makes it harder but it doesn't make it impossible. I'm also a firm believer that things have a way of falling into place, they have a way of unfolding naturally and I'm a firm believer that if something is meant to happen, then against all odds, it will happen.

So if our story does not end here, I hope I'm still the same when you're back.

I hope I don't lose an inch of respect for you. I hope I can still admire your qualities whether you're near or far and I hope I can still go to you for advice and I hope you still care.

I hope that when we meet again, we can still look at each other the way we did before timing and distance got in the way and I hope that the time we spent apart would help us realize what we truly meant to each other.

I hope our story is not like all other short stories; I hope our story is long, full of plot twists, surprises, lessons and I hope our story has a happy ending.

I hope we can look back at that time as an intermission, not an ending. As a cliffhanger, not the end of a show and I hope we're meant to go our separate ways so we can reunite again stronger, wiser and more forgiving.

But if this is the end of our story; if this is all it will ever be, then I hope that when we meet again, we're both happy, I hope we can still wish the best for each other because we both know how much we struggled to find meaning, to find love and find *ourselves.*

If I see you again and I don't feel a thing, I hope there's no bitterness, no resentment, and no sadness. I hope we can be a reminder of how God sometimes brings two people together to heal each other and once they're both healed, they move on to better and bigger things.

Maybe healing is not the same thing as loving. Maybe other people heal you so other people can love you. Maybe we all improve each other for someone else.

But if this is the end of our story, then I want you to know that you are my favorite chapter, the chapter I will go back and read when I want to smile and the chapter I will go back and read when the story gets boring and I hope I'm your favorite chapter too.

If our story doesn't have a happy ending, I hope we're the chapter that led to it and I hope we are the reason why we started believing in happy endings again.

But if we are meant for each other, then I hope we're both still on the same page when we meet again, that we can pick up exactly where we left off and keep writing the rest of our story together.

YOU'RE STILL THE ONE I WANT TO TALK TO WHEN MY LIFE IS FALLING APART

You're still the first person I want to talk to when I hear bad news, you're still the only one I want to cry to.

You're still the only one who can make me feel better when things go wrong; I don't know if it's the sound of your voice or the words you say so eloquently or just the way you understand my silence when people struggle to understand my words.

You're still the only one capable of making me smile when my tears are pouring down, you're still the hand I want to hold when I can't even feel mine.

Because it's always the tough times that reveal to you who you need the most and it's no surprise that I need you.

I need you to tell me that it's going to be okay and if it's not, then at least you're with me.

I can't do this alone anymore. But with you, there's nothing I can't conquer.

You're still the only one I want to be alone with.

It's ironic that sometimes we wait for things to go wrong to know what's right. It's ironic that we have to come so close to losing people or losing ourselves to remember who we really don't want to lose.

You're still the one I'm afraid of losing.

And today, I surrender.

Today, I need you.

Today, I want to call you and tell you what I'm going through.

Today, I want you to listen to me.

Because no matter who shows up at my door to comfort me, I'll still knock on yours.

If you're the reckless decision in times of sadness, I want to be irresponsible.

If you're the mistake I make because I'm not thinking clearly, I want to be foolish.

If needing you is wrong, I don't want to be right.

TO THE ONE I'LL ALWAYS REMEMBER

If I never see you again
I hope you know what you meant to me.
I hope you know how much your words
changed me
and how much your stories
touched me.
I hope you know that every night with you
was a life-changing night.
If it wasn't for you,
I would've stayed stuck
alone in the dark.
If it wasn't for you
I would've stayed hidden inside my shell
waiting for someone to crack me open,
but you were able to crack me open
without even trying,
you were able to guide me to the light
without even knowing how dark it was inside.
If I never see you again,
I want you to know
that you were more than just a friend,
that you were a mentor,
that you were someone I looked up to.
Maybe I wanted more
but I think I got exactly what I needed.
You got me out of my darkness

and maybe that was your role,
maybe you were sent to help me find myself,
maybe you were sent to help me love myself
and maybe you were sent to *save* me.

If I never see you again
I want to thank you for saving me,
I want to thank you for showing me the light
and I want to thank you for dropping me off
at the right exit
so I can find my own way.

Thank you,
I can take it from here.

YOU WANT SILENCE
AND I WANT TO TALK ABOUT US

You want silence. You don't want communication. You don't want confrontation.

And I just want to talk about us.

I want to talk about how you felt when you first saw me and what you told your friends about me.

I want to know what you told your mom when she asked you who you were with.

I want to know what was on your mind the first night you texted me and how you felt when I responded.

I want to know if I took your breath way when you saw me wearing your favorite color and if even for a moment, you imagined how I'd look in a wedding dress.

I want to tell you about how I felt and how you made me feel when I first saw you.

I want to tell you about how I didn't want our conversation to end and how I was trying so hard not to like you.

I want to tell you what I told my friends about you and how they all fell in love with the idea of us together.

But I mainly want to know why—why we ended up like this.

I want to know how—how we went from wanting to love each other to breaking each other's hearts.

I want to talk about us, but now I know why you're so quiet. I know why your silence is louder than your words, it's because there's nothing to talk about.

There's no us.

I DECIDED TO USE ART TO
TELL YOU HOW I FEEL

Call me weak. Call me a coward. Call me a liar. But I just can't tell you how I feel. I tell the world how I feel about you but for some reason, I can't tell you.

So I did what I do best and turned you into art.

I turned you into a poem. I turned you into an essay. I turned you into a book.

I wrote about your features. I told the world about your smile. I told the world about your eyes. I told the world about your body and I told the world about your intricacies.

I wrote about our beginning, our time together and I wrote about our ending.

I wrote everything I should have told you when I had the chance.

I even traveled far away to forget you but I ended up writing a whole book about you.

I turned you into art because art is safe.

Art agrees with me.

Art is a good excuse to say it all and then claim that it's not real.

Art is safe because I can always say it's not about you but the truth is—it is about you. My art is about you.

Everything is about you.

I write about loving you and call it art.

TO THE ONE WHO ALWAYS READS
MY MESSAGES BUT DOESN'T REPLY

I want to text you and tell you that I miss you but then I stop myself because knowing you, knowing our history, I don't know if I'll get a response. I don't know if I'll ever hear the words I want to hear from you.

That's how messed up things are these days; it's normal to expect someone you care about to ignore a message with your deepest feelings or even worse, give you a cold response.

I think this is what makes it so hard to be honest with people, the fact that they can hurt you again when they don't reciprocate your honesty or when they just read your message then put their phones away—put your *feelings* away.

The fact that someone can shove away your feelings like they're nothing or reply with an emoji makes even the simplest acts such as reaching out complicated.

Because even if you miss me too, will you ever tell me? Or will it be just another message *'read'* but not understood?

Read but not felt.

Read but not reciprocated.

Read but ignored.

TO THE GIRL THEY ALWAYS PICK

I hope you know how hard I fought for his attention, only for you to come in and sweep him off his feet.

I hope you know he made me cry so many nights because he wasn't making any effort, but now I understand that he was making you smile instead. He was making the effort with you, everything I needed from him was given generously to you.

And maybe I don't want to ask you how you do it or why he picked you but I'd like to know if you appreciate it, if you know how many girls would love to be you, getting his love and affection.

I hope you know that you broke so many hearts by winning his. I hope you know that every time I see you with him, I ask myself if you know how lucky you are, if you know that you're with a special man—a man I wanted to love.

You look like the kind of girl who'd break his heart, the kind of girl who would not understand his scars or his wounds or even listen to his stories and maybe that's why he picked you.

Maybe he picked you because he has never been loved the way he should have been and so all he knows is a love that is not real, a love that is not genuine and a love that doesn't last.

So while you have him, cherish every second he couldn't give me, appreciate every text he wouldn't send me, be fully present on every date he never took me out on and just try to love every part of him I wanted to love.

Try to kiss his wounds and run your fingers through his broken heart. Please feel it. Feel it beating for you and protect it. *Protect it from yourself.*

I don't know why he picked you and I don't know why you always stand in my way but I hope it's because when the right one comes along, you'll stay far away, you'll not be a barrier anymore because even if you were so close, he won't see you, you'll be invisible to him because he'll only have eyes for me.

I'll be the one he picked and the one he'll always pick no matter how many girls like you stand in my way. I'll be you for a change.

I HOPE THIS TIME YOU STAY

I hope that when we meet again, the years have changed you.

I hope you learned what it means to love. To stay. To stop running.

I hope you found love and lost it, so you know how much it hurts to lead people on.

I hope you got heartbroken a few times, so you can stop breaking hearts and try to fix them instead.

I hope you excelled in your career only to realize that it will never be enough for you.

I hope you traveled the world and saw things that startled you.

I hope that you had enough lonely nights to realize that sometimes all you need is someone by your side to get you through another day.

I hope you've done everything you've ever wanted to do, everything you claimed you need to experience before you settle down, everything that ever stopped you from fully loving someone else.

And I hope this time, when you find me again, you realize that you've been around the world and you met beautiful people but your heart always searched for me.

I hope this time, you look at me and see what I've seen all along.

I hope this time, you know for sure.

I hope this time, you smile and stay.

TO THE ONE I CAN'T GET MYSELF TO LOVE

I'm sorry I can't picture us together the way you do.

I'm sorry that every time we hang out you're on cloud nine and I'm stoic.

I'm sorry that I break your heart every time I talk about him.

I'm sorry I can't see you the way I see him.

I'm really sorry.

I know what it's like to be you. I know what it's like to be the one who cares more.

I hope you can move on.

I hope you tell yourself what you tell me. That you deserve someone who is sure about you. Someone who puts you first.

I hope you tell yourself that I'm not the one for you.

I hope you tell yourself that you shouldn't wait for me or anyone else.

Life is twisted like that. You want me, I want him and he wants her.

It sucks though, because while I talk to you about him and he talks to me about her, you're probably talking to her about me and we all wish they could just turn around and see us the way we see them. We all wish it was someone else loving us.

And I'm sorry that I know that and I still can't do anything about it.

I'm sorry I can't change my heart. I swear I would have asked it to beat for you.

THE THEORY OF US

I have a theory. It's complicated. But you will understand it because you like complicated things.

It goes something like this: I liked you and you liked me, then no one did anything about it. Then we did and it fell apart so we decided not to do it again.

Then I went on and liked other people and did something about it but they also kept falling apart.

And you went on and liked other people and you broke a few hearts along the way.

Then I decided I don't want to fall for anyone again because it just hurts.

And you decided that there are better things to worry about in life.

So I focused on myself and became the best person I could be.

And you focused on yourself, worked hard and made your parents proud.

Eventually, we'll meet again and this time, you'll be the best version of you and I'll be the best version of me and somehow, we'll magically be the best people for each other.

You had to be you and I had to be me so we could be us.

It's complicated, I know.

And the good news is that you don't have to believe it or agree with me because it's just a theory.

It's just my theory.

TO MY BEST FRIEND

Thank you for your loyalty. Thank you for being just as loyal when I'm not around. Thank you for letting people know that our friendship is not just another social media show because it's real. Thank you for not allowing strangers or people we barely know to get between us or even try.

Thank you for being my voice. Thank you for saying the words I would've said and saying them better. Thank you for speaking up when you could've stayed quiet. Thank you for not letting my absence change the way you feel about me.

Thank you for your love. Thank you for being kind to me even when people are being unkind. Thank you for reassuring me that you'll always be there for me no matter who tries to tear me apart. Thank you for seeing the best in me even when I don't even see it in myself.

Thank you for being in my life. Thank you for choosing to stay in my life, thank you for not being passive when it comes to me or our friendship. Thank you for keeping all your promises, for being there during the hard times, for celebrating the good times, for helping me out when I'm helpless and for being my voice when I can't speak. Thank you for showing me what friendship really is and thank you for showing everyone else what it means to be a true friend.

Thank you for loving me no matter how the years have changed me.

Thank you for allowing me to change, for allowing me to grow and for reassuring me that you'll always be there for the good and the bad.

Thank you for everything you've done and everything you still do.

But more than anything, thank you for making me feel safe in knowing that wherever life takes me, I can always come back to you. I can always find a *home* in you.

Thank you for reminding me that even though a lot of people will break my heart, you never will. Thank you for giving me the hope I keep looking for in everyone else.

Thank you for being there. Thank you for being present.

Thank you for staying in a world where everyone leaves.

I WAS WRONG ABOUT YOU; YOU'RE NOT THE GUY FOR ME

You're never going to be the one who shows up when I'm in pain at 3 AM to hold my hand and spoon me with love and affection. You're never going to be the one who goes out of his way to comfort me or stay with me until I fall asleep. You're not going to hold me in your arms until you make sure everything is alright again.

You only know how to be absent. You only know how to make me feel alone.

You're never going to be the person who makes me feel like I'm enough because you'll always be looking for something else, curious about someone else because you think you can do better. You'll never think I'm the best.

You're never going to be my Prince Charming. You're never going to be the person that's genuinely proud of me.

You'll never be the one who cares more or the one who stays. You'll never be the one who loves unconditionally or gives without thinking twice about it. You'll always be the one who's scared, the one who keeps making excuses.

You'll always be the one who breaks my heart.

You're never going to be my hero. The one who saves the day. The one *chooses* me every day. The one who puts me first. The one who understands that loving me may not be easy but it will be worth it and the one who knows that life will never be perfect but it's better when I'm in it.

Maybe I was wrong about wanting you to be in my story until it ends. Maybe your story ends here. It ends tonight. *It ends with me realizing I deserve the love I've been waiting for. The love I always believed in. The love you made me forget.*

It ends tonight because I want to remember how to be loved and maybe that's something you just can't do. I don't want your pain to change me. I want your pain to teach me how to love harder.

TO HIM (THE ONE I'M WAITING FOR)

Some days, I'm mad at you. I'm mad because it's taking you too long to show up. I'm mad because I thought you would come into my life five years ago. I'm mad because you're too late. I'm mad because I keep wishing for you and you seem so far away—so out of reach.

Some days, I find comfort in knowing you exist. You give me hope. You make me want to work on myself and become the best person I could be for you. All these lonely nights will make me appreciate your presence even more. All these heartbreaks will make me value your love even more. You make me want to keep going when I feel like giving up. You make me want to live when I feel like dying.

Some nights, I miss you. Why is it taking you so long to find me? How much longer do I have to wait? Do I know you? Are you a friend? Are you a stranger? Are you an old lover? I miss you and I don't even know who you are. But you've been gone for so long and my life has been so dull without you. I miss your calls every night and your texts every morning. I miss your wisdom and your tenderness. I miss your young spirit and your big heart. I miss your sense of humor and your chivalry. *I miss your love.*

Some nights, I feel like giving up. It's like I can find anything in the world but I can't find you. It's like you're that elusive dream I can't seem to reach. It's like you're the one thing I can't get right. The only one I can feel but can't touch.

I worry sometimes that you're never coming, that I'm just never going to meet you, that it's just not in the cards for me. I fear that it's always going to be just me against the world.

I fear that my fairy tale begins and ends with me.

But some days, I can feel it. Your presence. Your touch. Your smell. Your heart. Your soul. Your face. I can see it all so clearly. I believe in you more than I believe in anything in my life. I believe it because I prayed for you. I asked God for you. I suffered for you. I cried for you. I wrote for you. I lived for you. I traveled the world for you. And I can just feel it.

I'll find you or you'll find me. It doesn't matter. As long as you don't leave when you do.

And maybe you're late but the best things in life are worth waiting for. The best things in life don't come easily. The best things in life take time. And I can just feel it.

You're worth all the time in the world. You're worth the wait. You're worth the tears. You're worth all the heartbreaks.

Some days, I just know. That you're the one and when it's meant to be, we'll find each other and we'll just know.

Because I've been waiting all my life for you and you've been dreaming all your life about me.

DEAR GOD,

Dear God, when I run out of patience, please teach me how to wait and how to be strong while waiting, teach me how to be happy when I don't get what I want and teach me how to let go when you take something away from me. Teach me how to accept my fate without trying to turn it around.

Dear God, when I don't understand your plans, please try to explain to me why things had to be hard or why I had to suffer, please reassure me that you have spectacular plans for me and bigger things waiting for me.

Dear God, when I stop calling your name, when I stop praying, please don't hate me for it, find ways to bring me closer to you again softly and gently.

Dear God, open my heart to you even when it's breaking, let me find the light in the darkness, let me find hope in despair and let me find you when I feel like you're so far away.

Dear God, please don't let me get attached to what's not meant for me. Don't let me get attached to something or someone that you plan on taking away from me.

I know your plan is unknown but until you reveal it to me, please make it easier. Don't let me hold on to what

I need to let go of. Don't let me fight for what I need to release. Do not let me desire what will eventually destroy me. Do not let me love those who will break my heart.

Dear God, please don't let my heart miss people who don't miss me. Don't let my heart long for the ones who left. Don't let my heart fall in love with someone who doesn't want to stay.

Please don't let me get attached to the things that keep me up at night, to people who leave me wondering and to places I'm not meant to live in. Bring me closer to what's meant for me and give me the courage to walk away from the things that will only hurt me.

Dear God, please don't let me invest so much in things or people I'm bound to lose. Don't let me want what's not mine. Don't let me build a future around what's *temporary*.

And please God, love me through it all. Love me through the confusion, the tears, the anger and the pain. Love me because your love heals me.

I have faith in you. I have faith in your kindness, your mercy, your forgiveness and your sympathy.

I have faith in what you've written for me. My story. My destiny. My *maktub*.

Dear God, I'm writing the best story I can write for myself, but you're the only one who can complete it. You're the only one who can finish it. So with all my heart, I put all my trust in you and I'm handing you the pen and I'm ready to go wherever you want to take me.

THE LAST ONE

I decided to live for myself.

I decided to be for myself everything I've been asking people to be for me.

I decided to share my story with the world.

I decided to be fearless.

I decided to take the road less traveled.

I decided to be the man of my dreams.

I decided to be the woman I've always wanted to be.

I decided to ask for the closure I never got.

I decided to tell people how I feel.

I decided to make peace with rejection and heartbreak.

I decided to try and fail.

I decided to use my voice.

I decided that I'll either write with honesty or not write at all.

I decided to love myself.

I decided to try to love my life the way it is.

I decided that as long as I'm alive, I'll try to make my days count.

I decided to believe in a brighter future.

I decided to forgive myself.

I decided to turn my pain into art.

I decided to write this book so I can start over.

I've said everything I've been wanting to say to everyone.

And now I need to figure out what I want to tell myself.

What I want my legacy to be.

What message I want to send to the world.

I decided to leave the last letter *open-ended*—because my story hasn't ended.

My story is just beginning.

My story begins now, after I released all that was weighing me down. After I've said all the words I should have said and written all the letters I should have sent

Now I'm free.

Now I'm reborn.

Now I'm healed and staring at a blank page.

My life has just begun.

Rania Naim grew up in Cairo, Egypt with more than just a passion for writing; it was her dream. Rania's passion for writing bloomed when she realized that she wanted to dedicate her time bringing personal stories to life. Her stories are all inspired by true events and by everyday conversations. As a writer for Thought Catalog, Rania writes about life, love, work and the pursuit of your best tomorrow.

twitter.com/Ranianaim
instagram.com/ranianaim
facebook.com/Ranianaimpage
ranianaim.com

THOUGHT CATALOG Books

Thought Catalog Books is a publishing house owned by The Thought & Expression Company, an independent media group based in Brooklyn, NY. Founded in 2010, we are committed to facilitating thought and expression. We exist to help people become better communicators and listeners in order to engender a more exciting, attentive, and imaginative world.

Visit us on the web at *www.thoughtcatalogbooks.com*

Collective World

Thought Catalog Books is powered by Collective World, a community of creatives and writers from all over the globe. Join us at *www.collective.world* to connect with interesting people, find inspiration, and share your talent.

MORE POETRY FROM
THOUGHT CATALOG BOOKS

All The Words I Should Have Said
—*Rania Naim*

Your Soul Is A River
—*Nikita Gill*

Seeds Planted In Concrete
—*Bianca Sparacino*

This Is For The Women Who Don't Give A Fuck
—*Janne Robinson*

THOUGHT
CATALOG
Books

BROOKLYN, NY